WALT DISNEY
·TREASURY·

First published in 1987 by
Octopus Books Limited,
59 Grosvenor Street,
London W1

Illustrated by Ayse Ulkutay

ISBN 0 86273 317 0
Printed in Hong Kong

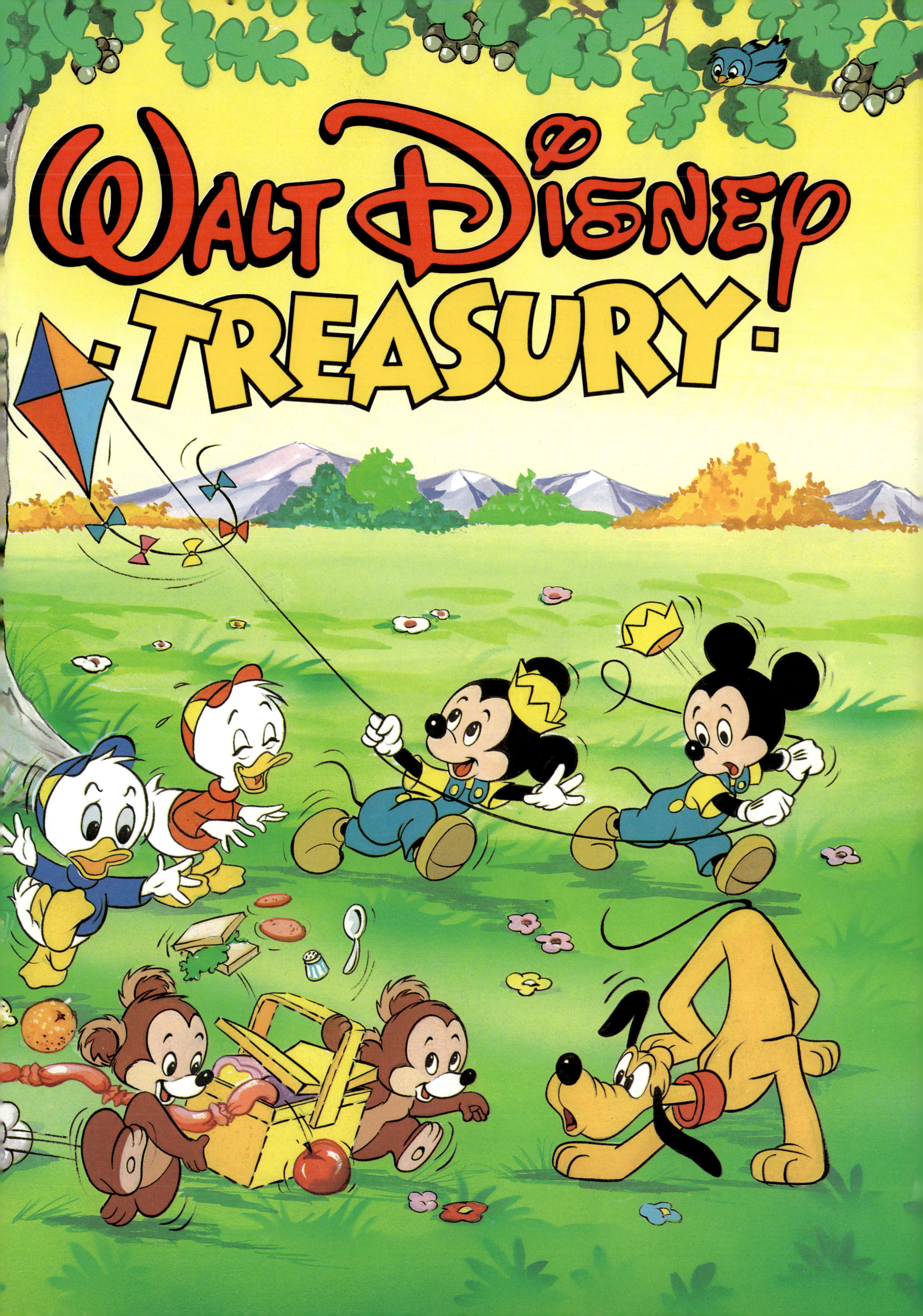
WALT DISNEY
TREASURY

CONTENTS

forth on the smooth, velvety grass. 'This is really living,' Donald decided. 'At home I always have to push the lawnmower myself.'

Just then, as the mower finished its work and shut itself up in the garage, the front door of the house swung open, and Huey, Dewey and Louie came out. They looked grumpy and crumpled, and Dewey had a bump on his foot.

'Uncle Scrooge's automatic pool cleaner chased me out of the pool,' complained Huey. 'And look what it did to my tail feathers!'

'Uncle Scrooge's solid-gold bowling balls are too heavy,' moaned Dewey. 'I dropped one on my foot!'

'Uncle Scrooge's TV has a time-guard tuner,' Louie reported. 'It won't turn on until six o'clock!'

Suddenly there was a click and a swoosh and a pitter-patter of very wet drops.

'Ughh!' shouted Donald. 'It's the automatic lawn sprinkler!'

Donald and the boys raced for the house. When they came dripping and splashing into the front hall, a panel in the wall popped open. Out came a little machine that waved a tiny mop. It made angry tick-tick-ticking sounds and chased the ducks up the stairs. Then it busily mopped the water off the floor.

'That gadget's angry with us!' shouted Huey.

'It swatted me on the ankle,' complained Louie.

'I wonder if we can even have a snack in this house without getting into trouble,' grumbled Dewey.

As it turned out, Donald and the

boys *couldn't* even have a snack without getting into trouble. They couldn't even have a snack *at all* – there was no refrigerator in the kitchen. There was only an electronic food server, which was set to serve dinner at seven o'clock and not a moment before. There was nothing they could do about it.

Donald and the boys waited and waited. At last the food server rang its bell, and the robot butler buzzed into the dining room carrying a tray of delicious food.

'Baked ham!' cried Dewey.

'And corn on the cob!' exclaimed Huey.

'Let's take our time and enjoy it,' said Donald. 'Remember, we won't be able to help ourselves to any snacks tonight!'

Huey, Dewey and Louie did take their time. In fact, they took too much time. Before they had finished, the robot butler buzzed in and picked up their plates. Then it buzzed back to the kitchen and clattered the plates into the instant-sud bowl which gurgled and churgled and washed them clean.

'But I'm still hungry!' wailed Louie.

'Listen!' said Dewey.

Outside by the front gate, a tune was playing. It sounded like the ice-cream van. Donald completely forgot that he wasn't supposed to let anyone in. He ran and pushed the button to open the electric gate. Then he and the boys dashed eagerly out on to the porch.

Did they see an ice-cream van driving up the drive? No. What they saw were three horrible burgling Beagle Boys, who trotted in, chuckling evil chuckles.

'Oh no!' cried Huey. 'They'll take the rubies out of Uncle Scrooge's swimming pool!'

'They'll steal the gold bowls out of Uncle Scrooge's bowling alley!' moaned Louie.

Donald leaped to the master control panel. He turned knobs. He twirled tuners. He twisted dials, and he clicked switches. All around Donald and his nephews, Uncle Scrooge's automated house began to buzz and hum and clank and rumble and tick. The little moppng machine popped out of the wall and chased a Beagle into the dining room.

There, the robot butler picked the Beagle up and carried him to the kitchen. It plopped him into the instant-sud bowl, which gurgled and churgled and covered the Beagle with suds. It was a frightful experience for the poor Beagle, who hadn't had a bath for over twenty years.

A second Beagle was trying to steal the rubies and emeralds from Uncle Scrooge's swimming pool, but the automatic pool cleaner came scrubbing along and chased him out. Then, when he ran into the house, the built-in super vacuum whooshed him into an opening in the wall. He stuck there fast, along with Uncle Scrooge's second-best umbrella and an old hat stand.

The third Beagle had got too close to the automatic pin-setter in Uncle Scrooge's bowling alley and it was picking him up and setting him down – and picking him up and setting him down – and picking him up and setting him down.

Fortunately, Uncle Scrooge came home early and rescued the Beagles. 'I'm proud of my marvellous house!' he cried. 'Those villains won't try to get in *here* again!'

'I don't think *we* will either,' said Donald. He and the boys climbed down off a bookshelf and hurried home to their own simple little house.

First, they had a nice snack from the refrigerator. After that, they watched television for a while. Then they went to bed and slept soundly all through the night. And who can blame them?

Pluto the Detective

Mickey and his dog, Pluto, lived together in a cosy little house. They were very good friends. Every morning Pluto ran out to get Mickey's paper, then they played tug-of-war with it. Mickey always let go first so Pluto always won. Sometimes they played go-fetch. Mickey threw a stick and Pluto ran after it and brought it back.

One day, Mickey was reading the newspaper when he saw something very interesting. 'Hey Pluto,' he said. 'Listen to this. The paper says there was a big jewel robbery yesterday. Fifty thousand pounds' worth of jewellery was stolen from Otto's Jewellers. The owner is offering a five-thousand-pound reward to anyone who helps find the jewels. I'm sure the two of us could track down those robbers,' he said. 'Help me find my detective outfit.'

Mickey put on his detective hat and coat. Pluto put on his fiercest look.

Then together they went outside and started searching. Pluto sniffed everything along the way and he kept his nose close to the ground so that he wouldn't miss anything. Suddenly he smelt something and started to run.

'Is it the robbers, Pluto?' asked Mickey.

But Pluto just ran and ran. He pulled Mickey along behind him till, forgetting about him, he jumped over a fence and broke his lead, and Mickey fell flat on his face!

On the other side of the fence, Pluto found what he was looking for. It was a bone. But then he saw Butch, the biggest, ugliest, fiercest looking bulldog in the neighbourhood, and the bone lay on the grass very near him. Pluto

thought he was fast asleep. He knew he shouldn't take the bone away from him, but it was too good to give up, and he picked it up very quietly. Butch opened one eye and growled.

Off ran Pluto with the bone in his mouth and Butch followed close behind. They ran down the street, round a corner and knocked over the greengrocer's fruit and vegetables, but they both kept running.

Pluto looked for somewhere to hide. He saw a door and ran through it, not knowing that he was going into the Hall of Mirrors! Inside he was surprised to see lots of other dogs. There were thin ones and fat ones; small ones and large ones and they were all carrying bones, just like him. Poor Pluto thought it was very strange. He didn't realize that they were all reflections of himself.

Just then Pluto saw Butch. He looked huge so Pluto ran off as quickly as he could. Still holding the bone between his teeth, he ran out of the Hall of Mirrors chased closely by Butch. He didn't look where he was going and bumped into a little girl. He got such a fright that he dropped the bone and that was the chance that Butch had been waiting for. He grabbed the bone and disappeared, but Pluto kept running. He ran on and on until he came to the park and only then did he realize that Butch was not chasing him any more. Feeling exhausted he looked for a place to lie down and finally curled up under a park bench where he fell fast asleep.

Later that evening, two men came into the park. One was short and fat, the other was tall and thin and they were obviously looking for something. The short man pointed at the park bench. 'I hid the package of jewels under there,' he said.

'You fool,' said the tall man, sharply. 'Somebody else has probably found it by now.'

The two men looked under the park bench and saw Pluto. 'There's the package,' one of them whispered. 'That dog is lying on it.'

Pluto was resting his head on the package and when the tall man reached for it, Pluto woke up. The man tried to grab the package but Pluto wanted to keep it and he bit into it and held on with all his strength.

Just then Mickey came into the park. He was sad and tired and had spent hours looking for Pluto. Suddenly, he heard him growling and whistled loudly for him. But Pluto did not hear him as he was so busy trying to hold on to the package of jewels. Finally, the two men lost their hold and Pluto trotted off feeling very pleased with himself. He had no idea that he was carrying the jewels. He saw Mickey and he ran to meet him. The men followed.

'That is our package,' they said to Mickey. 'Can we have it back?'

Mickey was just about to give it to them when they grabbed it. The string came loose and beautiful jewels began to tumble out on to the ground. Mickey immediately realized that they must be the stolen jewels and the two men must be the robbers. He blew his detective's whistle, and the two robbers were so busy picking up the jewels that they did not see two policemen running up to see what all the noise was about. The policemen were amazed to see the two men on their hands and knees amongst the jewels and arrested them straight away.

'Thanks, Mickey,' said one of the policemen. 'You and Pluto did a fine job. You have certainly deserved your reward.'

The next night, Mickey and Pluto sat quietly by the fire. Mickey had the five-thousand-pound reward and Pluto had a fancy collar and a delicious bone!

Donald Duck - Prize Driver

'Well, what did you learn at school today, boys,' Donald Duck asked his nephews one evening, when they got home.

'We're studying safe driving, Uncle Donald,' said Huey, Dewey and Louie.

'Good idea,' said Donald. 'That's what this country needs. Just watch me. I'll show you what safe driving is.'

'How did your car get dented Uncle Donald?' asked Huey.

'That was done by a very bad driver,' said Donald. 'I was going along at a good speed, minding my own business, when this car pulled right out in front of me. Boy! Was I furious.'

'Anger causes accidents,' said Louie.

'Now listen, you fellows,' said Donald. 'I was driving a car before you were born. You don't have to teach me! I'm going over to see Daisy now. Do you want to come along or not?'

'Of course, Uncle Donald. We'll come,' said the boys. They all hopped in and got out pencils and paper.

Donald glanced at his watch. 'Gosh, we're late!' he said. 'We must hurry.'

The first traffic lights turned amber as Donald drove up, but he sneaked through. The boys wrote in their pads.

When Donald tried to turn on to the busy main road, there was no gap in the traffic and no one would let him in.

'Look at these awful drivers,' Donald fumed. 'They never think of anyone else.' At last, he was so impatient that he stamped his foot on the accelerator and swung out in front of a car so the driver had to slam on her brakes. 'That'll show her,' Donald said, and the boys made a note in their pads.

'Now,' said Donald, 'we can make up some time,' and he zoomed off down the road, swapping from one lane to another and back again.

The boys hung on to each other and shut their eyes. 'Help! This is too fast!' they cried.

'You want to go slowly do you?' said Donald, in disgust, as he drove along in the fast lane. And without changing lanes, he began to drive very slowly. Cars lined up behind him and some tried to overtake on the inside. He

caused a terrible traffic jam, but without worrying about it, he drove on to Daisy Duck's house. The boys made a note in their pads.

When they got home, the three boys began whispering to each other. 'It's worse than we thought,' Donald heard Dewey say.

'Why are you three so gloomy?' Donald asked.

'Well, we have entered you in a contest at school for the most courteous driver in town,' said Huey.

'That's fantastic,' said Donald.

'But look at your record on that last journey,' said Louie.

'You drove through amber traffic lights,' said Dewey.

'You took a risk because you were angry,' added Huey.

'You wove from lane to lane on a busy road,' said Louie, 'and jammed up the traffic by driving too slowly in the fast lane.'

'But look at all the things I do right,' Donald snapped. 'I keep my brakes and lights working properly and I don't overtake on hills and bends.'

'Yes we know, Uncle Donald,' the nephews sighed. 'But for us to win the contest, you have to be the most polite driver in the town. And you're a long way from being that.'

'Oh I am, am I?' cried Donald. 'Well, I'll show you! I'll show the whole town.'

Next day, as Donald was driving the boys to school, he saw some cars waiting to turn on to the busy main

road. He slowed down and let some of them in. He drove at the speed of the rest of the traffic, staying in one lane most of the time. He was careful to park close to the curb and not take up any of the next parking space.

'Courtesy doesn't take much time,' the boys were quick to point out.

Donald politely opened the car door and bowed as the boys stepped out.

As the days went by, Donald found it was fun to be polite. He liked to see

people smile when he stopped at zebra crossings to let people cross the road. He liked to see lorry drivers wave their thanks when he stopped to let them turn right in front of him. He always signalled carefully when he was going to turn or slow down.

At last it was the day for the parents' meeting. Huey, Dewey and Louie took part in a safety drill while Donald watched from the audience.

'Goodness,' Donald whispered to Daisy at his side. 'Those kids are the best of the lot!'

Next, the headmistress introduced Sergeant Horsecollar of the police. 'The Sergeant will award the prizes in the courteous-driver contest we've been running in the town,' she said.

'It's a pleasure to be here,' said Sergeant Horsecollar. It's a long time since I was a pupil here, but we're never too old to learn. And one of the biggest lessons we can learn today is in driving. It pays to be polite.

'Tonight, it is my pleasure to award the prize for the most courteous driver in town to . . .'

Donald smoothed his feathers and straightened his tie, ready to stand up.

'. . . Mr Mac Turner, father of Sandy Turner of this school.'

'Thank you,' said Mr Turner from the platform. I drive a lorry, and anyone who drives all the time can tell you it pays, really pays, to take time to be polite.'

'Now,' said Sergeant Horsecollar, 'we have another prize to award. An even more important one, because it proves that we can go on learning even when we're grown up. The prize for the driver who has improved most in driving courtesy goes to the uncle of Huey, Dewey and Louie Duck – Mr Donald Duck!'

'Ladies and Gentlemen,' said Donald from the platform, 'I used to think it was clever to drive fast. But I've learnt that it's a lot more fun and more clever to take time to be polite. The credit belongs to my teachers, though. Huey, Dewey and Louie.'

So Huey, Dewey and Louie went up on the platform and each took a bow – one, two , three!

Clarabelle Cow's Easter Bonnet

It was Easter day and everyone was entering the Easter Parade. A prize was to be awarded for the best bonnet.

'Where's your Easter bonnet, Clarabelle?' asked Clara Cluck. 'We're all looking smart for the Easter parade. Even Horace Horsecollar has put a ribbon round his straw hat.'

'I did have a hat somewhere,' said Clarabelle. 'But I don't know where I've put it.' She hunted about until at last she found her hat in the barn, but it was squashed completely flat. 'Oh

bother,' she said to herself. 'I must have sat on it. I can't possibly wear it in the Parade now.'

'All line up!' crowed the cock. 'Everyone gather in the meadow, straight away!'

'We mustn't be late,' squawked Clara Cluck. 'Come along everybody.' She straightened her dandelion bonnet and bustled off.

Poor Clarabelle followed along behind the others. She was the only animal in the whole farmyard without an Easter bonnet. She was so upset about it that she didn't even go into the meadow with the others. She hid behind the hedge instead and tried to peer through a hole.

'Off we go!' cackled Clara Cluck, and the Parade began. The geese looked very smart in cherry blossom berets, and the pigs wore bright yellow buttercups round their blue hats. The

sheep came next but Clarabelle couldn't see them properly through the hedge so she made a bigger hole and tried to look through. But the hedge was thick with may blossom and it was very prickly. She tried a bit further along, but there it was full of wild roses and they were even more prickly!

At last Clarabelle found a small gap and pushed her head right through. There was a loud chirping noise but Clarabelle didn't take any notice. She was far too interested in the parade.

Just then, Horace Horsecollar marched past and he saw Clarabelle watching the Easter parade through the hedge.

'Clarabelle,' he said. 'Your bonnet is beautiful. May blossom, wild roses and a birds' nest on top with four little birds in it! I think you deserve first prize!'

'Hear! Hear!' shouted all the animals when they saw Clarabelle's bonnet. So Clarabelle was given first prize.

Clarabelle blushed. 'Thank you all very much,' she said.

'However did you think of it?' asked Horace.

Clarabelle blushed even more. 'It just sort of came to me,' she said. And only she knew how true that was!

Donald Duck's Christmas Tree

It was the day before Christmas. At Donald Duck's house all the cakes were cooked, the presents were wrapped and now it was time for the Christmas tree. Donald picked up his coat and hat and mittens. 'Come along, Pluto,' he called. 'We're going to the woods to find our Christmas tree.'

Pluto came running, and together they went into the snowy woods.

Now deep in those woods, in a sturdy fir tree, lived two merry chipmunks called Chip 'n' Dale. They were getting ready for Christmas too, and had found a tiny fir tree standing in the snow. They were decorating it with berries when Donald and Pluto came along. When the chipmunks heard Donald whistling and saw Pluto prancing they scampered back to their fir-tree home, where, they thought, they would be safe.

Donald Duck looked around in the wood for a suitable tree and when he saw the chipmunks' sturdy fir tree he said, 'This is just the tree for us.' Chop, chop went his axe and poor Chip 'n' Dale were too frightened to think.

Home through the woods went Donald Duck, dragging the fir tree behind him. Up in the branches sat Chip 'n' Dale, having a nice ride.

Donald set up the tree in his living room. From their hiding place in the branches, Chip 'n' Dale watched as Donald looped long strings of coloured lights over the branches. They watched him hang bright-coloured balls.

'There!' said Donald when the job was finished. 'Doesn't that look lovely,' and Pluto agreed.

'You stay here while I get the presents,' Donald told Pluto and he went out of the room. Pluto sat down to admire the tree.

As soon as Donald was out of sight, Chip 'n' Dale appeared. They danced on the branches till the needles quivered. They made funny faces at themselves in the shiny coloured balls and laughed till their little sides shook.

Pluto growled at them disapprovingly but Chip 'n' Dale didn't mind. Chip just picked off a ball and threw it at Pluto.

Pluto caught it in his paws. 'Grr,' he growled crossly.

Dale picked off another ball and threw it at Pluto. Poor Pluto jumped and caught it in his teeth and just at that moment Donald came back. 'Pluto!' he

cried. 'Bad dog! Now try to be good while I bring in the rest of the presents.' He didn't notice the two naughty chipmunks.

No sooner had Donald gone, than Chip 'n' Dale appeared again. Chip didn't look where he was going and his head went straight into a yellow ball. Dale laughed and laughed, but Pluto didn't think it was funny at all. 'Grr,' he growled, getting ready to jump.

'Pluto!' cried Donald Duck. 'What do you think you are doing? Do you want to ruin the tree?'

Just then, there was a crash and a tinkle and something fell to the floor.

'What was that?' said Donald.

Pluto pointed to the tree, and when Donald peered in among the branches he found Chip 'n' Dale. 'So you're the mischief makers,' he chuckled. 'And to think I blamed poor Pluto.'

Pluto went and opened the front door. He wanted Chip 'n' Dale to leave but Donald disagreed. 'Oh Pluto,' he said. 'It's Christmas Eve. We must be kind to everyone. We must let the chipmunks stay here.'

So Pluto made friends with Chip 'n' Dale. And when Mickey and Minnie and Goofy came round, they all sang carols, and everyone agreed that this was by far their happiest Christmas Eve ever.

The Kitten Sitters

One day, Morty and Ferdie, Mickey Mouse's nephews saw Minnie Mouse drive up to the house. She got out of her car holding something in her arms, and Mickey went out to meet her.

'Guess what!' said Mickey Mouse to his nephews, when they came outside. 'We're going to be kitten-sitters. Minnie is going to leave Figaro the kitten with us tonight while she visits her cousin, Millie.'

At that moment, there was a wild clucking and flapping and crowing from next door. Pluto came racing across the lawn chased by a big angry rooster. He rushed into the porch and hid while Mickey shooed the rooster back to his own garden.

'Pluto!' scolded Minnie. 'Chasing chickens again. Aren't you ashamed?'

Pluto *was* a bit ashamed, but only because he had been cowardly and let the rooster chase him. Creeping out from the porch, he wagged his tail and grinned sheepishly.

'I think it's a good thing Figaro is going to stay with you,' said Minnie to Mickey. 'Figaro is a little gentleman. He can teach Pluto how to behave.' With that, she handed her kitten to Mickey, got into her car and drove away.

Minnie had only just driven away, when Figaro jumped out of Mickey's arms and scampered into the house. He ran straight into the kitchen, where he saw a jug of milk on the table that Mickey had forgotten to put away. He jumped on to a chair, then up on to the table, making the jug wobble then topple over. Milk spilled all over the table and on to the floor, which was exactly what Figaro wanted. He started to lap up the milk and Pluto growled at him disapprovingly.

'Take it easy, Pluto,' said Mickey, wiping up the milk. 'Figaro is our guest.'

Figaro of course was very pleased when he heard that. He wrinkled his nose at Pluto and stuck out his tongue. Then he raced all around the house, even jumping into the ashes in the fireplace so that afterwards he left sooty footprints on the carpet.

'Figaro's a very *messy* little guest,' said Morty as he got out the vacuum cleaner and cleaned the carpet.

At dinner time, Pluto ate his dog food, like a good dog. But Figaro was very naughty. The boys tried to persuade him to eat the special kitten food that Minnie had left for him but he refused to touch it. Finally, he agreed to nibble at some sardines.

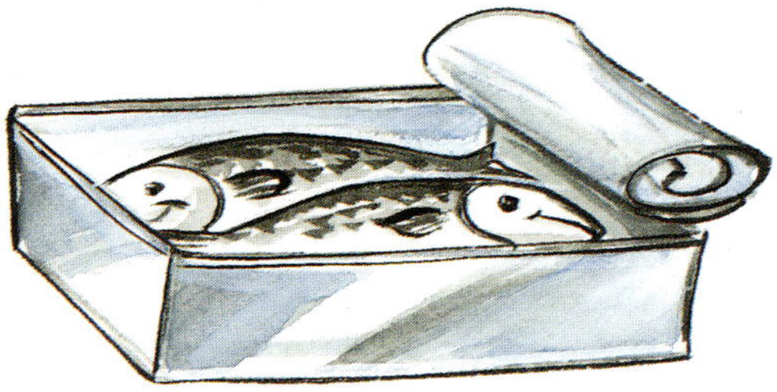

'He's a *fussy* little guest,' said Ferdie.

At bedtime, Pluto curled up in his basket as usual and went to sleep. Minnie had left a lovely soft cushion for Figaro to sleep on but he decided he didn't like it. Instead, he jumped into bed with Morty and nipped his toes. Then he got into bed with Ferdie and tickled both his ears. Finally, he scampered into the kitchen.

The house suddenly became very quiet.

'Uncle Mickey,' called Morty, 'did you remember to close the kitchen window?'

'Oh no!' cried Mickey, and he leapt out of bed and ran into the kitchen. The

kitchen window was wide open and Figaro the kitten was nowhere to be seen!

Mickey and the boys searched the whole house. They looked under the beds and the tables and the chairs. Then they looked behind every door and in every cupboard. After that they went out into the garden and looked under every bush and behind every tree. No Figaro.

'He's really run away,' Mickey said at last and he went back to the house. He put his coat on over his pyjamas. 'You two stay here,' he told the boys. 'Pluto and I will find Figaro. Leave the porch light on for us.'

Pluto did not like being disturbed. He didn't wag his tail, and he didn't even try to grin as he got out of his warm cosy basket. But off he went, without complaining, to help Mickey search for Figaro. They went to Minnie's house first, but Figaro was not there. Then they went to the park. 'Have you seen a little black and white kitten?' Mickey asked the policeman at the gate.

'I certainly have!' answered the policeman. 'He was by the pond, teasing the ducks.'

Mickey and Pluto hurried down to the pond. Figaro wasn't there either, but Mickey could see he had been there. He had left behind some small, muddy footprints and several very cross ducks.

Mickey and Pluto followed the trail of footprints down the main street. There they met some firemen. 'I'm looking for a black and white kitten,' said Mickey to the firemen.

'Is that so?' said one of the firemen. 'We have just rescued a black and white kitten. He had climbed a telephone pole and couldn't get down again. He ran through that alley.'

In the alley, a man was busily cleaning up some broken eggs in his van.

'Have you seen a kitten?' asked Mickey.

'Have I!' said the driver. 'He jumped into my van and broke lots of eggs.'

Mickey groaned as he paid for all the smashed eggs, then he and Pluto searched the whole town for Figaro. They even went to the police station but no one had seen him. When they finally got home, dawn was breaking.

'What will Aunt Minnie say?' asked the boys.

'I hate to think,' answered Mickey.

Later that morning, Minnie Mouse arrived at the house to pick up her kitten, and Mickey and the boys went out to meet her.

'Where is Figaro?' asked Minnie.

No one answered.

'Has something happened to him?' Minnie asked. She was upset and angry. 'Can't I trust you to look after just one sweet little kitten for me?'

Just then there was a loud clucking and squawking from next door. Several furious hens came flapping over the fence, and close behind the hens came the big, angry rooster. Close behind the rooster came Figaro, the kitten. He was dirty and scruffy and he had a long feather in his mouth.

'There's your sweet little kitten!' said Mickey.

'Figaro!' cried Minnie, not believing her eyes.

At the sound of his mistress's voice, Figaro quickly came to a stop in front of her. He sat down and mewed, trying to pretend he was a good, gentle little kitten. Then he began to wash himself as if nothing had happened.

'He ran away last night,' explained Mickey. 'He teased the ducks in the park and broke some eggs and . . . '

'And now he's chasing chickens!' finished Minnie. 'I hoped he'd teach Pluto some manners,' she went on. 'Instead, Pluto has been teaching him to do those naughty things. Teasing ducks! Chasing chickens! I dread to think what else. I'll never leave him here again.'

'It wasn't Pluto's fault!' protested Morty.

'He didn't do anything naughty,' added Ferdie. 'He stayed up all night, trying to find Figaro.'

But Minnie refused to listen to them. Without staying any longer, she picked up Figaro, got into her car and drove quickly away.

'Don't worry, boys,' said Mickey. 'We'll tell her the whole story later, when she's not so upset.'

'Please don't tell her too soon,' begged Morty. 'As long as Aunt Minnie thinks Pluto ia a naughty dog, we won't have to kitten sit with Figaro.'

Mickey smiled. 'Maybe we should wait a little while. We could all do with some peace and quiet. I did learn one thing though,' he said as he stretched out beside Pluto under a shady tree. 'There's not much time to sit when you're kitten sitting!'

Donald Duck's Fishing Trip

One day Uncle Donald took Huey, Dewey and Louie to the seaside. He took his fishing rod and some worms with him as he wanted to do some fishing.

When they arrived, Donald marched to the end of the pier. 'Now boys,' he said, 'you stay around here while I catch a fish for lunch. Then we will have a delicious barbecue.'

'But that means that we will have to wait till you catch a fish, before we can have lunch,' cried the boys. 'We're hungry now!'

Donald sat down on the end of the pier and cast his fishing line into the water. 'I'll catch a big fish in no time,' he promised happily.

But Huey, Dewey and Louie were not so happy. They could not stop thinking about food. And the more they thought about it, the hungrier they got.

After ten minutes, Donald had not yet caught a fish, and the boys began to think of what they could do. Just then, Dewey saw a boy walking by with a bird-shaped balloon.

'I've got an idea,' Dewey said, and he hurried off to some stalls on the beach. He looked around for a balloon seller and eventually found just the right balloon. Then he ran back quickly to the pier.

The three boys took turns blowing up the balloon. It grew bigger and bigger and bigger. It was shaped like a

large fish. The boys swam with the balloon out to the end of the pier, making sure that Donald didn't see it. They held it underwater and catching hold of Donald's line, tied the balloon fish to it. Then they gave a gentle tug on the line.

Donald felt the tug. 'A fish!' he yelled. And he began to pull in the line.

Underwater, the boys held on to the balloon fish. They felt Donald tugging at the line but they hung on. At last, Huey had to let go and he climbed out of the water up beneath the pier.

Then Dewey let go of the fish. Donald grinned as he pulled in what he thought was a large fish on the end of his line.

Finally, Louie could hold on no longer. He let go. SWISH! The balloon fish flew up out of the water. Huey was waiting for it and he stuck a pin in, making it shoot off.

Poor Donald was pulled off his feet. He tumbled over backwards off the pier and into the water.

Huey, Dewey and Louie climbed on to the pier and looked down into the water. There was a great splashing where Donald had fallen in. At last he came to the surface.

Louie called down to him. 'Hey, Uncle Donald. You're never going to catch a fish. Why don't you give up and we'll buy some lunch?'

But suddenly he stopped. His eyes opened wide. Huey and Dewey gasped. Donald was wading out of the water carrying the biggest fish the boys had ever seen. And it was a *real* fish.

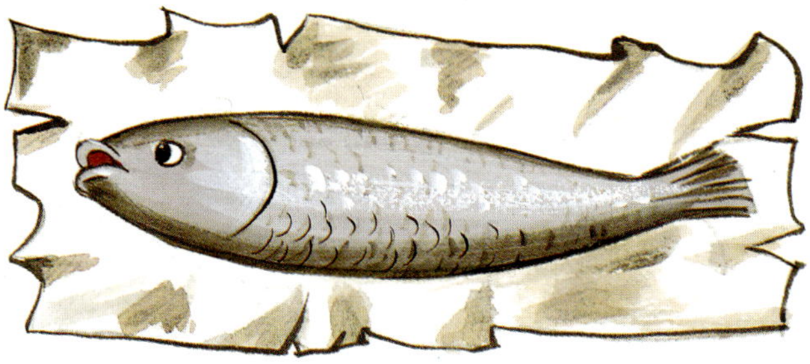

'I've caught that fish, boys,' Donald said. He was very pleased with himself and grinned happily.

Huey, Dewey and Louie smiled too. Although they knew it would take a long time to clean the fish, and a long time to cook it, they also knew that there was nothing in the world that tasted as delicious as barbecued fresh fish and they were happy to wait!

Grandma Duck's Green Fingers

Mr Hearwell, Grandma Duck's neighbour, always seemed to be in the right place at the right time to hear all the latest important neighbourhood news. One morning, when he picked up his phone, he had a crossed line and couldn't help hearing Grandma talking.

'Yes, Dr Feelingood,' Grandma was saying, *'I certainly do have green fingers.'*

Mr Hearwell was so startled that he almost dropped the phone. 'Green fingers,' he thought. 'That sounds serious,' Of course, he had to listen a little longer.

'A special spray. I think I can handle that,' Grandma continued. *'I'll be sure to follow your instructions exactly. Come right away if possible, and send schefflera and false aralia over as soon as you can. I think the palms will have to be sprayed, too.'*

'Oh my goodness gracious,' Mr Hearwell murmured to himself. 'The green is spreading all over her hands, and the doctor is sending all kinds of medicine! I'd better tell some of the neighbours.'

The moment Grandma hung up, Mr Hearwell began calling his neighbours. 'I'm afraid I have some very important and serious news about Grandma Duck,' he told everyone. 'Can you come right away?'

The neighbours were used to Mr Hearwell's phone calls, because he always had very important or serious news about something. But they all cared very much about Grandma Duck, so they hurried over. In no time at all, they were gathered in Mr Hearwell's kitchen.

'This is the worst possible news I could tell you,' Mr Hearwell said in a low, sad voice.

'There, there,' comforted one of the neighbours. 'Maybe it's no so bad. Why don't you tell us?'

'Well,' Mr Hearwell said, 'I just happened to hear Grandma talking to Dr Feelingood on the phone. Her fingers have turned green! She told him to come over right away. She even asked him to send all kinds of special medicine to keep the green from spreading all over her hands.'

'Goodness! That sounds dreadful,' said another neighbour. 'What should we do?'

'That's simple,' someone replied. 'Let's go over to see Grandma and ask if she needs anything.'

'Oh no,' Mr Hearwell said, trembling. 'The disease might be catching. We don't want to spread it around the neighbourhood.'

'That's true,' the neighbours agreed. 'Why don't we go down the road towards Grandma's house? When Dr Feelingood leaves her house, we can ask him how she is.'

Grandma's neighbours were in such a hurry that they got to Grandma's house before the doctor did. They hid behind a big tree and waited. Suddenly, they spotted a big truck, loaded with green plants, coming down the road. They all craned their necks, trying to see where the truck was going. It stopped right in front of Grandma's house, and the driver began carrying the plants inside.

'Oh dear,' groaned Mr Hearwell. 'Grandma must be terribly ill! All her friends and relatives have sent plants to cheer her up.'

'Maybe we should send her some flowers,' suggested a neighbour.

'Great idea! Come back to my house and we'll ring up and order some,' said Mr Hearwell. 'Perhaps they can be delivered right away.'

The neighbours spent the rest of the morning in Mr Hearwell's kitchen. They were so busy talking about Grandma's fingers that they never saw the flower van go by, delivering the lovely flowers they had sent her. Very soon, they were all surprised to hear the doorbell ring. They were even more surprised to see Grandma Duck herself standing on the doorstep holding a beautiful bunch of roses.

'Grandma, what are you doing here? You shouldn't be walking around,' they all cried. Of course they tried to catch a glimpse of her green fingers, but she was wearing gloves.

The neighbours quickly helped Grandma to a chair, put her feet up and tried to make her comfortable.

'Goodness!' exclaimed Grandma. 'Why shouldn't I be walking around? And what did I do to deserve all this? I just came over to thank you for the lovely flowers. What's the occasion?'

'They're a get-well gift from all of us,' explained Mr Hearwell.

'But I'm not ill,' Grandma said, looking very puzzled.

'Yes you are,' insisted Mr Hearwell. 'I heard you talking to Dr Feelingood about your green fingers and about sending medicine over. And then we saw you getting a lot of get-well plants.'

'Tee-hee,' giggled Grandma. 'Oh Mr Hearwell, you've done it again! Those weren't get-well plants. Dr Feelingood is going on holiday. He had heard that I've got green fingers, which means that I'm good at taking care of plants, and he wanted to know if I would care for his plants while he's away.'

'Well that certainly explains everything,' said Mr Hearwell, blushing. 'But at least you're OK, Grandma.'

'Yes I'm fine. Green fingers never hurt anyone,' said Grandma. 'I'd better return these lovely roses to you all.'

'Oh no,' cried the neighbours all together. 'Please keep them as a "we're-glad-it-was-a-mistake gift".'

So Grandma went home – roses, green fingers and all.

Madam Mim and the Beanstalk

One day, Scrooge McDuck gave his nephew, Donald, five tickets for the pantomime. Donald was astonished. Uncle Scrooge was usually so mean. He never gave anything to anyone.

Donald decided to take his three nephews, Huey, Dewey and Louie with him, and that evening they set off to the theatre. On the way, they met Madam Mim and asked her to join them. Madam Mim was thrilled!

When they arrived at the theatre they showed their tickets at the door. But the doorman pushed them outside. 'These tickets are for last year's pantomime,' he cried.

'Huh!' snorted Donald. 'That's typical of Uncle Scrooge.'

Huey, Dewey and Louie were very upset. The posters for *Jack and the Beanstalk* had looked so exciting and the boys had been looking forward to going.

'You shall go to the pantomime,' said Madam Mim, suddenly. She waved her wand and WHOOSH! they all found themselves inside the theatre, sitting in the front row!

The pantomime started and at last it was time for Jack to climb the beanstalk. But the beanstalk on the stage looked rather wobbly. Nevertheless, Jack bravely began to climb.

'Oh dear,' gasped Madam Mim. 'That beanstalk will never carry his weight!'

She took out her pocket spellbook and found a suitable spell. 'Izzy! Ozzy! Hear me talk. Grow and grow you feeble beanstalk.'

Hey presto! The beanstalk began to grow strongly. It grew and grew and grew. It sprouted giant leaves, and got thicker and thicker. Poor Jack was soon lost in the middle of it.

The beanstalk spread further. It was soon growing over the edge of the stage into the orchestra pit. It wrapped itself round the harp and crept into the trumpets.

Donald was terrified. 'Stop!' he yelled, but the beanstalk was creeping into the front row of the audience and had got hold of his hat. 'Change the spell,' he shouted at Madam Mim.

'I can't,' she spluttered. 'This book doesn't tell me how to do that.'

Donald fled from the theatre, followed by Huey, Dewey, Louie, Madam Mim and the rest of the audience. Once outside, they watched the beanstalk push its way through the windows. It had soon covered the theatre, inside and out.

'I must go home and fetch my monster spellbook,' cried Madam Mim. 'I must stop that beanstalk before it grows all over the town,' and she zoomed off on her broomstick.

Donald and his nephews went home in a bad temper. Their evening had not turned out as they had expected.

'Never mind,' said Daisy Duck, who was waiting for them. 'I've made you your favourite supper – sausages and green beans.'

'Beans!' they all howled. 'We never want to see a bean again – Never!'

Detective Mickey Mouse

Mickey Mouse sat in the office of the Mickey Mouse Detective Agency, reading mystery stories and waiting for a case to work on.

'Oh Pluto,' Mickey sighed. 'Perhaps, someday there will be an exciting book all about me – *Mickey Mouse in the Case of the . . .*'

Suddenly there was a knock on the door. Mickey could see a shadow on the other side of the frosted glass. 'I wonder who that can be,' he muttered.

The door opened slowly. The visitor stepped inside.

'Why, you're the famous actress Lola LaWow!' Mickey exclaimed.

'How sweet of you to recognize me,' the actress said. 'I've come to you because Tutu, my dear sweet poodle, is missing. You must help me find her. She was last seen at my mansion today at breakfast time. Where, oh where can she be?'

'We'd better start by looking for some clues,' Mickey said. 'Pluto, you stay here and guard the office.'

But Pluto wanted to go and look for Tutu too, so Mickey agreed to let him come.

Minnie Mouse was watering her garden when she saw a smart car coming down the street. 'Why, there go Mickey and Pluto and . . . Lola LaWow. Goodness!' thought Minnie, 'I wonder where they can be going in her big fancy car.' She decided to follow in her own car and find out.

When they had nearly reached Lola LaWow's mansion, Pluto suddenly started barking and he tried to jump out of the car.

'Pluto, sit!' Mickey commanded. 'I don't know what's got into him,' he chuckled, turning to Ms LaWow.

Meanwhile, Minnie stopped to read a big sign at the side of the road. It said, 'Sizzle Sausage Factory – Grand Opening Today!'

'Mmm, I bet those sausages taste good!' said Minnie to herself. Then she drove on.

At Ms LaWow's mansion, Mickey said, 'I'd better talk to all the servants. One of them may have dognapped Tutu.'

'But everyone loves Tutu,' Ms LaWow said. 'No one would . . .'

'Detective Mickey Mouse is on this case,' said Mickey. 'Bring in the first suspect.'

In came Peeves, the butler. 'The last time I saw her,' he said, 'Tutu was right by this door, whining and scratching to go out. But I don't have time to walk her *and* clean up the mud she trails all over the house.'

'Aha,' thought Mickey. 'He doesn't like cleaning up after Tutu. I bet the butler did it, just like in The Case of the Missing Mongrel.'

Minnie was listening at the window. 'Hmm,' she thought. 'Tutu must like being outdoors.'

Next Mickey wanted to question the chauffeur. The beautiful actress led the

way to the garage and Mickey followed. Minnie secretly followed too.

Inside the garage, the chauffeur complained, 'Walking Tutu is not much fun. Whenever we pass a butcher or a hot-dog stand, that little dog pulls at the lead till I buy her something.'

'This is like the Puzzle of the Parked Cars,' Mickey decided. 'It wasn't the butler after all. The chauffeur dognapped Tutu because he didn't like taking her for walks.'

But Minnie thought, 'Goodness, Tutu must really like meat.'

'You can see the cook next,' said Ms LaWow. 'This way to the kitchen.'

The cook told Mickey that she was tired of preparing fancy dishes for Tutu. 'All she ever wants are the sausages on Madame's breakfast tray,' the cook sighed. 'Tutu almost knocked me down this morning jumping for Madame's sausages. I had to carry the tray above my head.'

'In Mystery of the Merry Mousse, the cook committed the crime,' Mickey thought.

'That's the answer,' Minnie thought quickly. 'Tutu is crazy about sausages and she didn't get any this morning.'

'All this is too much for me,' Ms LaWow said, dabbing her eyes with her handkerchief. 'I must rest now. I'll leave you to find the gardener yourself,' she said to Mickey and she turned and went upstairs.

Mickey walked out of the door and into the garden.

'Hey! Watch out!' the gardener shouted. 'That's just what that little dog did – trampled all over my beautiful flowers!'

'So,' Mickey thought, 'the gardener is angry with Tutu too. They're all in this together. It's just like my favourite story – Case of the Crazy Kidnappers.'

Just then, Pluto sniffed the air excitedly and bolted off through the flower bed.

'Not again,' the gardener moaned.

'Pluto! Pluto, come back!' Mickey called after the disappearing dog. 'Where is he running off to? Now I've got two dogs to look for!'

'I bet I know where to find both dogs,' said Minnie, popping up from behind a bush.

'Minnie! What are you doing here?' Mickey asked.

'Solving the case,' replied Minnie. 'Someone has to, while you're busy flirting with that actress.'

'Oh Minnie. You know you're the only girl for me,' Mickey said.

Minnie smiled and grabbed Mickey's hand. 'Let's go and find those dogs!'

'If I'm right,' Minnie said, 'this small set of paw prints belongs to Tutu, and these larger ones are Pluto's.'

Minnie and Mickey followed the trail. Soon Minnie sniffed the air. 'Aha,' she said. 'Sausages.'

They saw before them the new Sizzle Sausage Factory. A big crowd was gathered for the grand opening. Suddenly, everyone burst into applause. Minnie and Mickey ran to see what the excitement was about.

'Why, it's Pluto!' Mickey exclaimed proudly.

'And that must be Tutu!' Minnie shouted gleefully.

The two dogs were doing funny tricks, and the manager of the factory rewarded them with fresh, plump sausages.

Mickey telephoned Ms LaWow. 'Your worries are over,' he told her. 'We've found Tutu.'

After a big sausage lunch, Mickey, Minnie and Pluto went back to the office to wait for someone to come in with another case to solve.

'Now that they want Tutu to be in the television commercials for Sizzle Sausages,' Minnie said, 'she'll be a star too!'

'I'm glad Tutu found a job. But I couldn't have found Tutu without you two,' Mickey told his friends and he had the notice on the office door repainted. Now it said, 'Mickey Mouse *and* Minnie Mouse Detective Agency. Pluto Hound for Hire!'

Donald Duck's Toy Train

Donald Duck was thrilled. He had a new toy train. It was a beautiful one and he had set it up in his back garden. It had a shiny black engine and a truck for coal. Donald had to ride in this truck because he was too big for the cab. The train had a coach, a mail van and a red guard's van. But none of Donald's friends could sit in the train because it was only a toy and much too small for them.

Donald had built a little station beside the track, and all around the station he had put a little village with houses and a church and a little shop. But nobody lived there, of course, because like the train it was a toy and too small.

One day, Donald was laying some new track. But there wasn't room for it all in his garden because there was a large tree in the way.

'This will have to go,' said Donald. 'It's much too big for my toy train.'

So Donald had it removed. He arranged for some tree fellers to come and chop it down.

Now, in the treetop was the home of two chipmunks, Chip 'n' Dale. Donald didn't know about them, and the tree fellers came when poor Chip 'n' Dale were away from home, out gathering nuts to store for the winter. When they came back, they had armfuls of nuts. They could hardly believe their eyes when they saw that their home had disappeared. Where the large old tree had stood, there was a toy-sized tree. Donald had put it there because it

was just the right size for his toy train.

'That tree isn't big enough for us,' cried Chip.

'It'll never do,' said Dale.

Where could they live now? The two sad chipmunks sat down by the toy track and thought, but they couldn't think of anything they could do. So they got up and started walking slowly down the railway track. Soon they came upon the train, just where Donald had left it.

'This could be fun,' said Chip.

'Let's go for a ride,' said Dale.

They climbed up into the engine cab, which was just the right size for them. Then they stoked up the fire with coal, and away they went, down the track.

As they chugged down the track, they came to the little village where they stopped at the station.

'This looks like a nice town,' said Chip.

'Let's look around,' said Dale.

They knocked on the doors of the little shops, and rang the bells of the little houses, but no one answered them. One little door was not shut though, and it swung open when Chip touched it.

Inside the house, they found tables and chairs, lamps and beds, just the right size for them. It was perfect for their new home, and they moved in there and then.

After a while, they heard someone coming up the road. It was Donald Duck and he was very angry. 'Someone has stolen my train,' he shouted. 'It's probably wrecked by now.'

Just then, he saw the train, standing at the station. When he went to investigate, he saw some tiny footprints. He followed the trail and it led him up to the little house where Chip 'n' Dale were in bed, fast asleep.

Donald went to the window and peered inside. When he saw Chip 'n' Dale his anger left him. The chipmunks looked so comfortable in their new home and they were just the right size.

Donald soon made friends with Chip 'n' Dale. He let them drive his toy train while he rode on the coach behind. 'It's always fun,' said Donald happily, 'to play with friends who are just the right size!'

Mickey Mouse goes Camping

Morty and Ferdie woke up one morning feeling very excited. Donald was taking them on a camping holiday that day. They leapt out of bed and began to get everything ready. They had lots of things to take with them and they helped Mickey pack them all into his car. There was a tent, sleeping bags, pots and pans, tins of food, a camping stove, suitcases, fishing nets – and two spades.

'What do we need the spades for, Uncle Mickey?' asked Ferdie.

Mickey wouldn't tell them. 'Wait and see,' he said mysteriously.

At last everything was packed and they were ready to go. Minnie Mouse waved them off. 'How long are you going for?' she giggled, looking at the overloaded car. 'A year?'

But Mickey and his nephews ignored her comment and just waved goodbye. Off they went, and Mickey drove right out into the country.

When they had found a good camping spot Mickey stopped the car.

They all piled out. Morty and Ferdie grabbed their fishing nets and headed for the nearest stream.

'Hey! Come back!' yelled Mickey. 'Come and help me unpack the car.'

So the boys had to stay to help Mickey. Together they put up the tent, hammering in tent pegs and tightening guy ropes. It seemed to take hours.

'Can we go fishing now, Uncle Mickey?' the boys asked at last.

'No,' said Mickey, handing them the spades. 'You haven't finished yet. Now you are going to find out what the spades are for. You are going to dig a ditch all round the tent. Then, if it rains, all the water will collect in the ditch and not in our tent!'

The boys were dismayed.

'I don't call digging ditches much of a holiday,' grumbled Ferdie.

'Neither do I,' sulked Morty.

But Mickey stood and watched them until the ditch was finished. He was only satisfied when the ditch was so wide they couldn't even step over it, and it was so deep that it was deeper than they were tall. They would have to scramble in and out of it to get to or from the tent.

At last Mickey said they could go fishing. They rushed down to the stream and Mickey followed with his fishing rod. 'I'll catch something for supper,' he boasted.

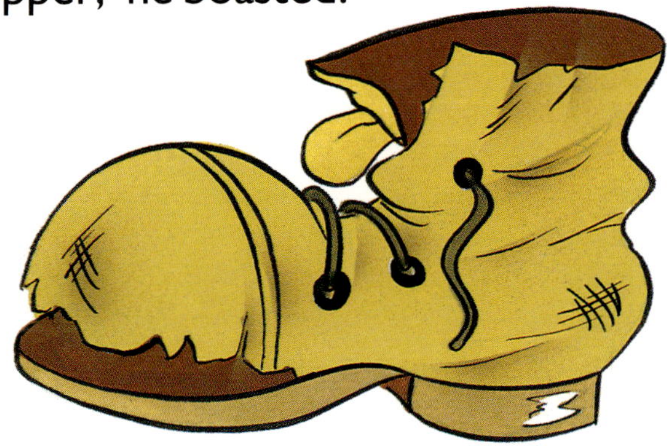

They fished for several hours, and all Mickey caught was an old boot. They would have starved if they had had to rely on him. Instead they opened a few tins, mixed everything together in a frying pan, and had a delicious supper.

Before long, Morty and Ferdie began to yawn. They were tired from all the fresh air and their hard work. So they scrambled into their sleeping bags and settled down for the night. Thunder rumbled in the distance and soon they heard heavy drops of rain falling on the roof of the tent.

Mickey smiled to himself. He didn't mind how hard it rained. 'I bet you boys are glad we dug that ditch,' he said proudly. 'Now we won't get wet at all.'

They all slept soundly through the night, but it was still quite early when Morty and Ferdie were woken by Mickey. 'Up you get, lazybones,' he shouted. He threw back the tent flaps and rushed outside. Morty and Ferdie heard a loud splash.

'Help! Glug . . . glug . . . glug . . . Help!' spluttered Mickey.

Morty and Ferdie peered out of the tent. There was Mickey splashing about in the ditch, although it looked more like a moat now it was so full of water.

'I thought you said the ditch would keep us dry,' giggled Morty, and both the boys doubled up with laughter.

Mickey was furious. And to make matters worse, as the ditch was too wide for the twins to jump across, they used Mickey's head as a stepping stone!

Mickey dragged himself out of the ditch. He found a large towel in the tent and wrapped himself up in it. 'Next time we go camping,' he groaned as he sat shivering in the towel, 'we'll take a caravan.'

'Oh no,' said Morty and Ferdie together. 'We love camping.' And waving happily, they ran off with their nets to do some fishing.

Donald the Brave

It was a beautiful sunny day and Donald and Daisy were out in the garden.

'I'd do anything for you, Daisy,' Donald was saying. 'I'd climb the highest mountain. I'd cross a raging sea. In fact I'm so strong and brave, I would even rescue you from the jaws of a man-eating tiger.'

'Oh Donald, you are wonderful,' Daisy said. 'I do admire a brave duck.'

Neither of them noticed Huey, Dewey and Louie watching from their bedroom window. They were giggling as they listened to the conversation in the garden. Louie suddenly had an idea and he told the others. Then they all giggled again.

'What a good idea Louie,' Huey said. 'It would be fun to make Donald prove how brave he is.'

Dewey nodded to Louie and Huey. 'I think our rocking-horse could become quite a good fierce tiger,' he said.

The three of them set to work. They found some paint and other odds and ends and began to change the rocking-horse into a tiger. They took off its saddle and bridle. Then they padded it with newspaper to make it the right shape. They painted it in orange and black stripes and stuck two knitting needles in either side of its mouth, for whiskers. Finally they gave his face the fiercest expression they could imagine.

When it was ready, Huey, Dewey and Louie carried the tiger into the garden and hid it behind a bush. They tied some rope to its front legs and put their plan into operation.

From behind another bush, Louie and Dewey pulled on the rope with all their might while Huey made fierce tiger roars. The tiger started to move slowly towards Donald and Daisy.

Donald was still boasting. 'I'd even save you from the jaws of a man-eating tiger,' he said, forgetting that he'd said that before. But his words turned into a terrified squawk when he saw a real live tiger coming towards him. It was roaring very angrily and it had a very fierce expression on its face.

'Help!' screamed Donald, and he took to his heels and made for the nearest tree. The tiger followed him and came to a stop right underneath the tree. Daisy meanwhile had fallen to the ground in a faint.

Huey, Dewey and Louie stood and watched as Donald scrambled up the tree. Once in the safety of its branches, he rocked backwards and forwards in fear and looked down at the tiger.

'It's all right, Uncle Donald,' called Louie.

'You can come down,' said Huey.

'We thought you would like to prove to Daisy how brave you are,' said Dewey. 'We made a fierce tiger out of our old rocking-horse.'

Donald was very embarrassed. He gulped once or twice in shame as he came down from the tree, and the boys felt rather sorry for him.

'Perhaps we can help him,' said Huey, and he told the others his plan.

Together, they pulled the rocking-horse tiger to where Daisy lay on the ground, gradually recovering. They quickly removed the rope and the rockers and rolled the tiger on to its side. Donald stood proudly with his foot on the fierce beast while his nephews hid the rockers and the rope from Daisy.

But poor Donald didn't get quite the reaction he was hoping for. When Daisy saw Donald she was not at all impressed. 'Call yourself brave!' she cried. 'You can't even capture one little tiger without the help of those three boys,' and she stormed off in a rage.

'Well,' said Donald in a huff, 'there's no pleasing some people.' And he went sadly into his house.

Huey, Dewey and Louie were pleased though. They were having a lovely time riding on the tiger, and they were wondering who they could scare with it next!

Mortie and Ferdie go Christmas Shopping

Mortie Mouse dried the breakfast things. Ferdie Mouse swept the floor. They both made their beds and picked up their clothes. Today was the day Uncle Mickey and Aunt Minnie had promised to take them Christmas shopping, if they were good.

They all went into town in Uncle Mickey's car. What a wonderful day it

was! There were snow flakes spinning in the air. There were frosty breezes blowing around the buildings. At every street corner bells were tinkling and every shop window was twinkling with coloured lights.

Best of all was the big department store. Mortie and Ferdie took Mickey and Minnie firmly by the hand, and led them through the crowd, straight into the crowded shop.

What a hustle and a bustle! What a clatter! What a crowd! But Mortie and Ferdie knew where they were going. Whenever Mickey Mouse or Minnie Mouse tried to stop to look at sweaters or mittens or socks, Mortie and Ferdie tugged at their hands and pulled them on. They had seen a sign saying TOYS, and they went straight to the toy floor.

What a wonderful place it was. There was a room full of dolls, but they raced past that. There was a room full of games and balls and bats and skis. But Mortie and Ferdie had no time for those. 'What we want for Christmas are things that go!' they shouted, and they raced on to the toy cars and trains, and some extra-special toy aeroplanes.

'Stay with Uncle Mickey while I go and do some shopping,' Minnie whispered to Mortie.

Mickey wanted to buy a present for Minnie too. 'Stay with Aunt Minnie,' he told Ferdie. 'We'll meet at the car at closing time.'

So there were Ferdie and Mortie on the great big toy floor all on their own. And what a wonderful time they had! They tried out every single toy that moved. They bought tickets for the space ship which advertised 'Quick Trip to the Moon'. And during the thrilling ride through space, Mortie and Ferdie fell asleep.

At the end of the ride, the other children piled out. The pilot climbed out of his space suit and stretched. 'I'm glad this day is over,' he said to Father Christmas who had also been in the shop that day. Then he went home. And all the assistants in the entire shop went home.

Suddenly, Mortie woke up. He looked around. It was dark and strange. 'Where are we Ferdie?' he asked.

'In the space ship,' said Ferdie, waking up too. 'Maybe we're on the

Moon.' So they opened the door and peered out.

There was the toy department, but how strange it looked now. For everything was shadowy and still. There was plenty of space in which to drive the toy cars and trains, but the boys did not seem to care.

Just then, they saw a beam of light. 'Let's see what that is,' they whispered, both at once. So hand in hand they tiptoed towards the light.

When they reached the open door, they peered through. Imagine their

and took them each by the hand. Then down through that big, quiet, empty department store they marched with a lovely, loud clomping sound. Through the big front door they saw Mickey and Minnie Mouse.

'Wherever have you been?' cried Minnie.

'Here they are,' said Father Christmas, 'safe and sound.' Then he turned to the boys with a serious look. 'Next time you're out shopping, you will remember to stay close to the grown-ups won't you?'

surprise. There sat Father Christmas.

'Well, well,' he said, when he saw them. 'What brings you here at this time of day?'

Mortie and Ferdie told him what had happened.

'I see,' said Father Christmas with a wise and kindly nod. And he stood up

'Yes sir,' said Mortie and Ferdie Mouse. And they really meant it. Next time they wouldn't let Mickey and Minnie go shopping on their own.

'See you on Christmas Eve,' called Father Christmas as he waved goodbye. 'And a merry Christmas to you all!'

Donald Duck – Super Salesman

It was market day and Donald Duck had promised to take Huey, Dewey and Louie shopping. They strolled down to the town and were soon walking through the stalls admiring all the things for sale.

The triplets watched the salesmen. They were very good at their job and Donald's nephews were impressed.

'Anyone can do that,' bragged Donald. 'It's easy.'

'*You* couldn't,' said Louie.

'You couldn't sell an overcoat to someone who was freezing!' said Huey.

'I bet you a week's pocket money that you couldn't be a successful salesman,' said Dewey.

Donald accepted the bet and that afternoon he bought lots of things that he was sure people would want. He then found a strong suitcase in the attic in which to carry them all and set off on his sales trip. 'I'll go to Daisy first,' Donald told the boys.

Huey, Dewey and Louie went along too, to see how he got on. When they got to Daisy's house, Donald spent a long time telling Daisy how wonderful all his goods were. He offered her a hat, a brooch, a scarf and lots more.

Daisy looked at everything and tried a pretty bow in her hair. 'I'd love to have this, Donald,' she said, 'but I can't buy it. I don't have any money.'

Donald felt sorry for her and wanted her to have the bow, so he ended up giving it to her.

Next stop was Mickey Mouse's house. They found Mickey cleaning his car and Donald tried to sell him a new key ring.

'Yes, I'll have one,' said Mickey.

Donald took one out of the suitcase, but as he was giving it to Mickey, he dropped it and it fell down the drain.

'Oh, no,' he said. 'I haven't got another one.'

Then Donald and the boys went to the baker. Donald was getting a bit worried. He hadn't sold anything yet. Huey, Dewey and Louie felt sure they were going to win the bet and would soon get an extra week's pocket money.

In the baker's Donald showed all his goods again.

'I could do with a new tie pin,' the baker said. 'How much is it?'

Donald smiled. He was so pleased that he'd sold something at last, that he bought a big cake for tea. But when they added up the cost of the pin and the cost of the cake, Donald realized that *he* had to pay the *baker* money.

Later that day, Goofy looked in Donald's suitcase. All he wanted to buy was the cake, but because he didn't have much money on him, Donald sold the cake for less than he'd paid for it.

Now Donald was worse off than he had been when he set out. He was very dejected and thought he would have to admit to his nephews that he wasn't a very good salesman after all. But, just then, a man carrying a suitcase dashed across the road to catch a taxi. As the taxi drew up, the man tripped over the kerb. His suitcase flew out of his hand, and split open on the pavement.

'Oh no,' groaned the man, looking at his broken suitcase. 'I have to be at the airport in half an hour. I'll never make it if I have to get another suitcase.'

Then Donald had a bright idea. 'You can buy my case,' he suggested. 'It's very strong and reliable and you would easily get all your belongings into it. But you'll have to buy the contents as well.'

'Agreed,' said the stranger. He was in such a hurry that he stuffed a handful of notes into Donald's hand without counting them or agreeing on a price for the suitcase. 'That should cover everything,' he said. Then he tipped everything out on to the pavement, crammed all his own things into it and climbed into the taxi. 'Thanks,' he said. 'You've been a great help,' and he went roaring away towards the airport.

When they all got home, Huey, Dewey and Louie watched as Donald counted the money.

'Well what do you think of that, boys?' Donald said. 'I call it a very handsome profit, and I've still got nearly everything I started out with!

'I told you it would be easy,' Donald went on. 'You should have known I'd make a good salesman.'

Huey, Dewey and Louie groaned. They wouldn't make a bet with Uncle Donald for a while.

'And by the way,' added Donald, holding out his hand. 'Don't you three owe me something too?'

Letters for Uncle Scrooge

Although Uncle Scrooge enjoyed getting letters, he hated bills even more than most people did. Uncle Scrooge was the richest duck in the world, but he really hated spending money! So, when Chives, the butler, brought in the post on a silver tray, Uncle Scrooge always flew into a terrible rage if there was so much as one small bill.

But this morning was different. There were no bills on the tray, but there were three letters – one each from Uncle Scrooge's great-nephews, Huey, Dewey and Louie. They had gone camping.

As Uncle Scrooge took the letters from the tray, he said excitedly, 'Stay Chives. Listen to the letters my great-nephews have written to me.'

'Certainly, sir,' replied Chives.

'I'll read Huey's letter first,' said Uncle Scrooge, ripping open the first envelope.

The letter said:

Dear Uncle Scrooge,
This camping holiday is great fun! I am really enjoying myself. My favourite activity is walking along the paths near where we are camping. I'm having a lovely time but I think Dewey and Louie might be a little homesick.
Love, Huey.

'It sounds as if Huey is having a wonderful time, doesn't it Chives?' said Uncle Scrooge.

'Indeed sir,' answered Chives.

'But poor Dewey and Louie,' Uncle Scrooge said. 'I was afraid that the great outdoors might be too much for them to handle. Let's see what poor little homesick Dewey has to say.'

Uncle Scrooge tore open the second letter and read:

Dear Uncle Scrooge,
Wow! Camping is fantastic fun! The weather is great. I could stay here forever, but I'm not so sure about Huey and Louie. They both seem to be a bit homesick.
Love, Dewey.

'Hmm,' said Uncle Scrooge, raising an eyebrow. 'It sounds as if Dewey is enjoying himself too.'

'Possibly, sir,' said Chives.

'Well, poor Louie. Poor, lonely Louie. Let's see how unhappy he sounds in his letter,' said Uncle Scrooge. He read:

Dear Uncle Scrooge,

What a lovely time I'm having here! Sleeping in a tent is such fun! The best part of camping is being able to watch the wild animals all around our camp. I'm having such a good time that I may never come home.

Love, Louie.

PS Huey and Dewey are really homesick.

Uncle Scrooge was silent for a moment. Then he said, 'Chives, I think each of of my nephews is homesick, but really won't admit it. What should I do? I wouldn't like them to give up and come home. Camping really is good fun and it's good for them to rough it.'

'If I might make a suggestion, sir,' Chives said. 'I believe your nephews would be less homesick if they could talk to you. Perhaps you could put in a phone system.'

'Drat!' exclaimed Uncle Scrooge. 'That would cost money. These letters might as well be bills!' Then he cleared his throat and said, 'Of course, I'll spend money to make Huey, Dewey and Louie happy.'

'Sir,' replied Chives. 'If you will allow me, I believe I can make a telephone that will cost you almost nothing.'

Uncle Scrooge cheered up. 'Try, Chives. By all means, try,' he said.

An hour or so later, Chives returned. He was holding a tin can with a string dangling out of the end. 'Sir,' he said to Uncle Scrooge, 'your nephew Huey would like to speak to you. Simply speak his name, rather loudly, into the can.'

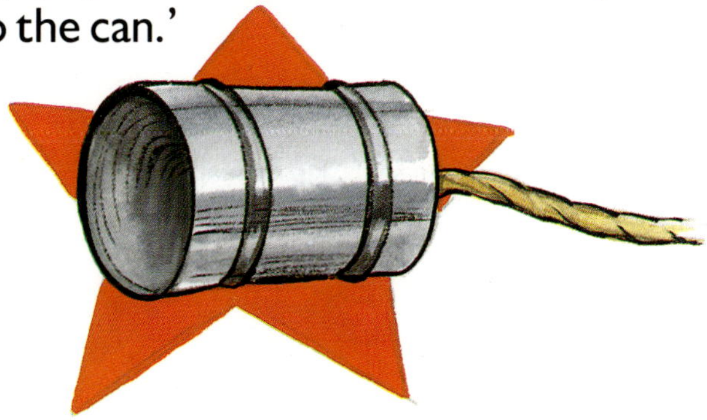

'Speak into the can?' Uncle Scrooge asked. 'How could that possibly work?'

Before Uncle Scrooge could say any more, he heard Huey's voice calling out of the can, 'Uncle Scrooge! Uncle Scrooge!'

Uncle Scrooge quickly grabbed the can from Chives and spoke into it. 'Huey! Huey! How are you?'

'I'm fine!' answered Huey's voice through the can.

After a long conversation with Huey, Dewey and Louie, Uncle Scrooge was beaming. 'Congratulations, Chives,' he said. 'Your telephone is a tremendous success!'

'Thank you, sir,' Chives said humbly, 'but I was lucky. If your nephews had been camping further away, I could not have stretched a string to reach them. Thank goodness they are camping in your back garden!'

The New Birdhouse

Huey stood back to admire the small birdhouse he had just put up on a tree. 'We'll soon have wrens singing around here,' he said.

'That really is a beautiful birdhouse,' said Uncle Donald.

'It's pretty good,' agreed Dewey, 'but no wren will ever get through that little hole.'

'it does look a bit small,' said Donald.

'I made the hole exactly the right size,' protested Huey. 'I'll bet you a million pounds that we'll have wrens in there.'

'One million pounds is a bit much,' said Donald, 'but I'll bet you next week's pocket money that by next week, no wren will have got through that hole.'

'It's a bet,' said Huey, and they shook hands to make the deal.

'But remember,' warned Uncle Donald, 'no cheating. It's up to the birds to decide who's right.'

That evening, while Uncle Donald and the boys were eating supper, two wrens came fluttering up to the birdhouse. They circled round the tree and twittered and chirped to each other. They took turns trying to get inside.

'It's such a lovely house,' sighed one of them.

'Yes, it looks fine,' chirped the other wren, 'but we can't live in a house that we can't get into.' And they flew away.

Early next morning, the wrens came back. But this time they had a friend with them. It was a woodpecker. Uncle Donald and the boys did not hear the rat-a-tat-tatting at the little birdhouse as the woodpecker pecked away at the small hole, making it larger.

After breakfast, Huey, Dewey and Louie went outside to look at the birdhouse.

'Uncle Donald,' called Dewey. 'Come and look. We've got wrens in our birdhouse.'

And sure enough, a little wren with a piece of straw in her beak flew easily through the hole.

Uncle Donald was very surprised but a bet is a bet. 'Well, Huey, I suppose I was wrong this time,' he said as he reached for his wallet. 'I was sure you had made that hole too small though.'

Donald and the boys did not notice the woodpecker that watched them from a nearby tree, and to this day, Donald doesn't know what really happened. The nephews don't know either, but the wrens are still living happily in Huey's birdhouse.

Pluto goes to Sea

'Why can't you be a hero like that ship's dog?' Mickey Mouse asked Pluto one day.

They were standing beside an ocean liner. On the deck lay a huge dog, staring proudly out to sea.

'There was a story in the paper all about the lives he's saved,' said Mickey. 'Why can't you be a dog like that?'

If all you had to do to be a hero was to lie on a ship's deck staring out to sea, Pluto was willing to try it. So Pluto went up the next gangplank they came to.

Mickey did not miss him for a few minutes. Then he whistled and called and looked all around, behind crates and barrels and in coils of rope. But not a trace of Pluto could he find. High above, on the deck of a large white ship, Pluto was sitting all alone, looking proud and haughty, gazing out to sea.

No one on the ship knew that Pluto was on board until they had left the harbour for open sea. There the waves rose and fell, and the ship pitched and tossed, and Pluto was as unhappy as a dog can be.

Down below, the sailors shuddered when they heard the dismal moans that came from the deck above. They went up to find out what was making them, and soon found the stowaway. They led him to a corner of the dark hold, where they made him a bed of old rags.

'It's a pity he isn't an intelligent dog,' said the second mate to the first. 'We could do with a watchdog to guard the captain's jewels.'

'Shh!' The first mate put a finger to his lips. 'No one must know about those jewels!'

It was too late , although they did not know it. A tough-looking sailor, who had found Pluto, had heard them talking. 'Aha!' he said. 'Them jewels will line my pockets soon and I'll jump ship at the very first port we come to, or my name is not Burglar Bob.'

Next day, Pluto's nose led him to the galley, where the ship's cat lived with the cook. The cat hissed at Pluto and arched her back. Pluto took off, racing for the deck. The cat chased after him, but she was travelling so fast that as the ship lurched, she slid across the deck, under the rail and down into the sea.

Pluto leant over for a better look and skidded, with a yelp, right after her!

When the sailors rescued them, they thought that Pluto had jumped in to save the cat. They called him a hero. They fussed over him and the mates moved his bed into the captain's cabin. 'He's just the dog we need to guard the captain's jewels, in spite of his looks,' they said.

Pluto did not like being shut in the cabin, though. He started howling so loudly that the captain shouted for the mates. 'Take that dog away. I'd rather be guarded *from* him than *by* him!' he cried.

So Pluto went back to his first spot on deck, from where he looked proudly out to sea. He kept a sharp look out for anyone about to fall overboard, because he liked being thought of as a hero.

That was the night that Bob had picked to steal the captain's jewels. The ship lay close to the shore and Bob had arranged for some friends to meet him in a boat. He slipped down to the cabin where the captain lay asleep. He hit him on the head with a truncheon and then stole the jewels!

With the jewels safely stowed in a small leather pouch, Burglar Bob signalled to his friends on the shore. When a small light answered, he kicked off his shoes, dropped the truncheon next to them and dived over the rail into the dark waves below. Splash! He landed and started to swim.

But Pluto had heard that splash too. One of his friends must have gone overboard! Time to be a hero again. 'Arf arf arf!' he barked, and he jumped into the sea.

'Man overboard!' the lookout yelled.

The sailors came running, turned the searchlight on, and soon saw Pluto and Bob floating in the water below.

When they were back on board, Bob was still complaining to himself about his bad luck, but out loud he said, 'I saw the poor dog slide in,' he claimed, 'and I couldn't bear to think of him drowning, so I jumped in to save him, of course.'

'Is that so?' said the first mate. 'Then what were you doing with this here truncheon that you left here near your shoes?'

'Wait a minute . Where's the captain?' the second mate cried. And he ran to the cabin to see.

Bob knew then that his crime would be discovered. 'Let me go!' he cried, and he ran for the rail.

But Pluto did not want another bath in the cold water that night! He made a frantic jump for Bob's trousers and hung on to them!

Soon the second mate was back, with the captain on his arm. The captain had a large lump on his head.

'Put Bob in the hold,' the captain said. 'And we'll get you a medal sir,' he went on. He was speaking to Pluto!

So, when the ship came home at last, Pluto was sitting proudly up on deck. And he was wearing a big shiny medal which said 'Our Hero' on it.

Mickey was wandering down by the docks, looking for his lost dog. He had done this every day since Pluto had disappeared. As the ship came up to the quay, Pluto saw Mickey. 'Arf!' he cried.

'Pluto!' cried Mickey. 'Why are you sitting up there? Where have you been? And why are you wearing a medal? What does it mean?'

The sailors told Mickey the whole story – how Pluto had saved the cat and then caught Burglar Bob stealing the jewels.

'I don't suppose you will want to come back home after all that,' said Mickey, after hearing the story.

But for his answer, Pluto gnawed his medal off and laid it at Mickey's feet. He still thought the best thing of all was to be Mickey Mouse's dog!

Donald Duck's Picnic

One sunny day, when Donald was strolling through the town, he saw a beautiful bright red, shiny bicycle in a shop window. He wanted to buy it although he hadn't ridden a bike since he was quite a small duck.

Donald remembered how much he had enjoyed riding a bike when he was young. He remembered all the places he had been. He could almost hear his old silver horn. What fun he had had blowing it at everyone as he passed!

Donald looked through the window again at the bike. 'I must have it!' he decided. But then he thought about his nephews, Huey, Dewey and Louie. What would they do?

Then Donald had a brilliant idea. He rushed into the shop and didn't come out again for three hours. When he did come out, he was wheeling his new bike – but it had four seats instead of one. Now Donald and all his nephews could ride it together.

Donald rode his new bike all the way home. When the triplets saw him they were thrilled. They wanted to try it straight away but Donald said they would have to wait till the next day.

'Let's go to bed now,' said Huey.

'Then tomorrow will come more quickly,' said Dewey.

'Come on then,' said Louie.

The three nephews rushed off to bed, but they were so excited they hardly slept a wink.

The next morning, very early, Huey, Dewey and Louie jumped out of bed and ran into the garden. It was a lovely sunny day and they couldn't wait to try out the new bicycle. They made such a terrible noise, trying to persuade Donald to get out of bed that Donald had to come down before they woke all the neighbours.

'Let's go,' shouted Huey.

'Let's take a picnic,' said Dewey.

'Let's hurry up,' said Louie.

Together, Donald and his nephews prepared a delicious picnic. They filled the picnic basket with sausage rolls, sandwiches, chocolate, bananas, milk shake, fizzy lemonade and cake. Then they put the basket on the carrier at the back of the bike and off they set.

Donald of course rode in front, then came Huey, Dewey and Louie. And it wasn't long before Donald realized his big mistake. He had been clever to think of four seats but he had forgotten to get four sets of pedals. He therefore had to do *all* the pedalling himself.

The countryside was very hilly. It was great fun whizzing down the hills at great speed, but going uphill was not such fun. Donald groaned as he pedalled up the hills, sweat dripping off his forehead. It was very hot and he began to wish it wasn't such a sunny day.

Huey, Dewey and Louie were enjoying themselves though. As Donald was doing all the hard work they had time to look around and admire the countryside. But, after the third hill, Donald had had enough. 'Let's stop here and have lunch,' he said. 'I'm starving already and if we eat now there will be less to carry later on.'

They all climbed down off the bike and looked for the picnic basket. It had gone!

'Oh no,' cried Dewey.

'It must have fallen off,' said Huey.

'We'll have to go back and find it,' said Louie.

Poor Donald's heart sank. He looked back down the road he had just come along and groaned. He didn't much like the thought of climbing up those three hills again, but he had no choice.

So, they all clambered back on to the bike and had just set off again when they heard a long SSSSS! Donald looked down and saw what he had hoped he would not see – a flat tyre. So, they all clambered off again and Donald set about mending the puncture. He found the hole and patched it up. Then he put the wheel back on the bike and fixed the pump to it. He was pleased that at least he had had the sense to buy a good pump with the bike.

'Not long now,' he said as he began to pump. But it seemed to be rather hard work pumping and Donald became hotter and hotter. His nephews crowded round him to watch.

'Get out of my way,' Donald squawked crossly. 'You're not helping by standing so close. I can't see what I'm doing.' He worked away at the pump but nothing seemed to happen.

The triplets began to giggle.

'Hee, hee, hee,' laughed Huey. 'You've got your foot on the air tube.'

Donald glared furiously at his nephews and took his foot off the tube. When he began pumping again, the bicycle tyre soon inflated and they were ready to go.

They all climbed back on the bike once more and Donald began to pedal home. He was very tired and to make it worse, Huey, Dewey and Louie were feeling very hungry and had began to squabble loudly. Along the country lanes, even the cows and sheep stared as the noisy ducks went by. Donald wished that he'd bought an ordinary bike and had left his nephews at home.

As they went along, Donald kept an eye open for the picnic basket. But it was nowhere to be seen and soon they were bicycling up their street. When they came in sight of their house they all saw the basket at last. It was there on their front lawn. It must have fallen off just as they had left home.

Donald felt very faint when he climbed off his bike and he mopped his brow. 'Let's stay here and have our picnic,' he gasped.

But Huey, Dewey and Louie had already tucked into the picnic. 'Come on Uncle Donald,' they all cried. 'There's not much left.'

Donald didn't have to be asked twice. He sat down with the triplets and helped himself to a large sandwich. And they all agreed they had never eaten anything so delicious as this picnic on their front lawn!

Donald Duck-
Private Eye

'Help!' cried Minnie Mouse. 'Mickey, my jewel box is missing. I can't find it anywhere. Someone must have stolen it.'

'Now, now,' said Mickey. 'Keep calm, Minnie. I will help you find it.'

Together they searched Minnie's house, upstairs, downstairs, and even in the garden. There was no sign of the jewel box.

'Oh dear. Oh dear,' sobbed Minnie. 'What shall I do?'

'There is only one person who can help us,' answered Mickey, 'and that person is Donald Duck, the great Private Eye. I will go to him at once and ask him to help.'

Donald was in his office and as usual, he was very busy.

'Donald! Donald! Wake up!' said Mickey. 'Minnie's jewel box is missing. We need you to help us find it.'

Donald opened a sleepy eye. 'I'll solve the mystery, Mickey,' he said. 'I'll search the underworld tonight and find the jewel box in no time.'

It was midnight when Donald entered the underworld. He didn't want to be recognized so his coat collar was pulled high, and his cap was pulled low to hide his face. He carried all his detective tools.

It was dark and spooky, and glittering eyes watched him from under lowered curtains. Donald was so busy searching for clues that he didn't notice a huge figure hiding in the deep shadows. Then as he moved into the darkness, a huge shadow tiptoed silently after him.

'I'll find Minnie's jewel box,' Donald said aloud, 'or my name isn't . . . '

'Donald Duck, the great Private Eye,' a great voice boomed out.

Donald leaped into the air with fright, dropping his tools.

The voice went on: 'That's not a very good disguise you have there, Donald.'

'Everybody can recognize you in that outfit,' added Pete kindly. 'Better try another disguise.'

'I will,' said Donald, 'and nobody will ever see through it.'

The next morning, Donald looked through all his books about disguises, but he didn't find any that he liked. Then he happened to look in a mirror. 'That's it!' he chuckled. 'I've found the answer. First, I'll fluff up my feathers and add a hair ribbon. Then I'll put on a blouse and skirt and a pair of tight high-heeled shoes! Then nobody will know me from *Daisy* Duck.'

Donald smiled proudly as he walked out of the door of his house, disguised as Daisy Duck. His three little nephews were playing marbles on the pavement. 'Hello, Uncle Donald,' they all shouted.

Donald stopped in his tracks. He was

As the moon came out from behind a cloud, Donald saw that the voice belonged to Pete.

very surprised that his nephews had recognized him. 'I suppose my disguise isn't quite perfect yet,' he thought. 'I'll have to try a different one.'

Back he went to his disguise cupboard. 'There,' he said after a few minutes, 'now nobody will know me from *Grandma* Duck.'

Just as Donald was coming out of his front door, Goofy walked past. 'Hello, Donald,' he said gaily.

Poor Donald!

'How did Goofy see through my disguise?' he asked himself as he changed his disguise. 'This time nobody will know me from Scrooge McDuck!'

Just then, Mickey and Minnie Mouse came running down the street, 'Oh Donald,' they called, 'we've found Minnie's missing jewel box. Morty had borrowed it to keep his fishing worms in.'

'I'm glad you've found the jewel box,' sighed Donald, 'but how did you all see through my disguises? I thought they were perfect.'

'They were almost perfect,' said Mickey, 'but you always forgot one thing. Uncle Scrooge would never be without his spats, Daisy's long eyelashes were missing and so were Grandma Duck's shoes.'

Poor Donald was very disappointed. He went inside again and decided to go back to looking like *Donald* Duck!

The Big Bear Scare

'It's a beautiful day to go camping!' Mickey Mouse exclaimed as he locked the front door of his house. 'Are you sure we have everything?'

'We're all ready to go, Uncle Mickey!' cried Morty. 'Ferdie and I have packed all the pots and pans and everything we could possibly need.'

'We've been ready to leave since daybreak!' added Ferdie excitedly.

'And I've packed enough food in my rucksack for three days, Mickey!' Goofy said. 'At first, I couldn't get it all in, but I finally found room for everything.'

Mickey smiled. 'That's great! I'm glad we've all planned so carefully for this trip. The tent's ready to be put up as soon as we get to our campsite.'

'Uncle Mickey, let's follow the new track out to the lake,' suggested Ferdie.

'Okay, boys,' Mickey agreed.

The day began well. Sunshine warmed the breeze, and the birds sang

happy songs. After a while, the friends stopped to eat some blackberries that Goofy spotted growing beside the path.

'I think this will be the best camping we've ever done,' Mickey told his friends.

As Goofy turned around to agree, he tripped over a log and sprawled on the ground. His bulging rucksack came open, and everything in it tumbled out on to the grass.

'Oh, no!' Goofy groaned. 'You fellows go on and find a good campsite. I'll repack this stuff and catch up as soon as I can.'

'Okay, Goofy. We'll set everything up, ready to start cooking when you get there with the food,' Mickey said.

'See you later!' the nephews called.

While Goofy scrambled to put his pack together again, someone just out of sight watched with quiet interest. A hungry mother bear had come to visit her favourite patch of blackberries. She stood behind a bush, only a few metres away from Goofy. Then, when his back was turned, she snatched the largest package from the ground and disappeared behind the bush again.

A few minutes later, Goofy hurried to catch up with his friends, scratching his head in bewilderment. 'This time everything fits into my rucksack perfectly,' he mumbled. 'I wonder why.'

'Hello, Goofy!' Mickey greeted his friend at the campsite. 'Why don't you start supper while I finish setting up the tent? I've almost done it.'

'We've already unpacked the pots and pans, Goofy. We'll help you!' said Morty and Ferdie eagerly.

'Mountain air really makes you hungry, doesn't it, boys?' said Goofy. 'We'll have fish tomorrow, but tonight we'll have the steaks I brought in my pack!'

Thinking how delicious the steaks would taste, Goofy hurriedly opened his rucksack. 'Here are the giant marshmallows – and the bread – and the peanut butter – and the pancake mix. And here –' He stopped suddenly. 'The steaks! The steaks are gone!'

'They can't be!' Mickey exclaimed.

'I must have left them at the place where my rucksack fell open!' explained Goofy.

'Well,' Mickey said, 'that's not so bad. We'll just follow the path back there and get them. Come on! Let's hurry!'

The four campers ran down the path. When they came to the blackberry bushes, however, the missing steaks were nowhere to be found.

'I've spoiled our best camping trip,'

Goofy said sadly. 'How could I have lost them?' He would not be comforted, no matter what Mickey and the nephews said to him.

Meanwhile, at the camp, three uninvited guests had arrived. The same mother bear and her two cubs had come to visit. The cubs quickly discovered that banging pans together

was fun. Their mother decided that the tent made a cosy place to sleep and settled down comfortably inside it.

'What's that noise?' Mickey wondered as they returned to their camp. Cautiously they hid in the bushes nearby and peered into the clearing.

'Oh, no! Bear cubs!' Ferdie moaned.

'Shh!' warned Mickey. 'Maybe they'll leave soon. It's strange that they haven't eaten those marshmallows yet.'

Suddenly Morty realized what must have happened to their steaks. 'I don't think they're hungry!' he said. 'They must be the ones who took our steaks!'

'Uncle Mickey,' Ferdie whispered. 'Look! Something's moving inside our tent!'

'Grrrrr,' rumbled the mother bear softly as she turned over to lie on her other side.

'It must be the cubs' mother,' Mickey said worriedly. 'How will we ever get her out of there?'

'I have to do something,' Goofy thought, 'otherwise, our whole trip will be spoiled – and it will be my fault.'

He noticed a bucket of water standing near the pile of firewood, and it gave him an idea.

While Mickey and the boys watched anxiously, Goofy crawled out of the bushes, straight to the bucket of water. He had never moved so quietly and carefully in his life. Grasping the bucket, he slowly made his way back into the bushes. 'Now,' Goofy thought as he hid behind a large tree, 'I'll climb this tree and throw the water on the bears. A shower should scare them away!'

However, the cubs had seen the bucket disappear into the bushes and were watching for it to reappear. Soon they saw the bucket moving slowly and awkwardly up the side of a tree trunk! Then the mother bear woke up and came out of the tent to see why the cubs were so quiet.

Climbing the tree was more difficult than Goofy had imagined. 'I must be high enough now,' he thought as he reached for an overhead branch. He peered around the trunk and prepared to take aim. And what did he see? He saw all three bears staring right at him!

Goofy was so frightened that he lost his grip on both the branch and the bucket of water. 'Help!' he cried.

CRASH! SPLASH! Leaves, branches, bucket and water, and Goofy all plunged down, flattening the tent! Startled, the mother bear decided that she and her cubs had had enough of this strange place. They ran off, quickly disappearing into the thick woods.

'The bears have gone! The bears have gone!' all four campers cheered with relief.

Safe beside the campfire that evening, Morty said, 'We've had an exciting day!'

'Goofy's pancakes taste almost as

good as steak,' Ferdie added contentedly.

'And Goofy found just the right way to send the bears home,' praised Mickey. 'He saved the whole trip!'

'Oh, it was nothing,' Goofy said shyly, but he had a grin from ear to ear as he spoke. After all, it isn't everyone who can scare away not one, not two, but three bears – all by himself!

Donald's New Toy

It was a very rainy day and Donald was bored. Huey, Dewey and Louie were quite happy to stay inside and read their comics, but it was difficult to concentrate. Donald was pacing up and down because, he said, it helped him to think better.

'I know!' he exclaimed suddenly. 'I'll take you to the toy shop and buy you each a new toy.'

'And one for yourself,' said Huey as they went out.

'Oh don't be silly,' replied Donald. 'I don't play with toys!'

Huey, Dewey and Louie were very excited when they arrived at the toy shop. There were hundreds of toys and they could not decide which ones they wanted. Huey ran around with a bright red plane pretending he was a pilot, but in the end he chose a racing car as he suddenly thought how much he'd like to be a racing driver. Louie admired a beautiful blue and white kite, but thought that since the weather was so bad he'd better choose something he could play with inside. So he picked a computer game.

Dewey could not make up his mind. He decided to ask Uncle Donald, who seemed to be enjoying himself more than his nephews!

'What about this lovely red hula-hoop?' suggested Donald. He liked the look of it himself.

'Well . . .' replied Dewey, thinking he preferred the space rocket, 'I . . .' But before he could say any more, Donald picked up the hoop, together with the racing car and the computer game, paid the assistant and marched the boys out of the shop!

'Oh dear,' thought Dewey. He wished he'd made up his own mind.

When they arrived home, it was still pouring with rain. Dewey was not very interested in his hoop. He stood it against the wall and played with Huey and his shiny green racing car instead.

At last it stopped raining. The boys pretended not to notice Donald pick up the hoop and slip out of the door. When he had gone, they clustered around the window to watch. They giggled as he spun the hoop and wriggled his hips. He tried and tried to keep the hoop spinning around his waist, but every time, no matter how hard he wriggled, the hoop just slid down to his feet and landed – BONK!

Donald became very annoyed. He picked up the hoop and stormed out of the garden.

'We'd better follow him,' said Louie. 'He's sure to get into trouble!'

They followed Donald. He walked fast up the hill behind their house, clasping the hoop very tightly. Donald was going to play at rolling the hoop down the hill. At first, the hoop just wobbled and fell over, but at last, off it went, gathering speed as it shot down the hill.

'That's the end of that!' groaned Dewey as his hoop whizzed past their hiding place. Donald came running after it, panting and puffing, but the hoop got further and further away from him.

'He'll never get it back now!' said Louie.

On went the hoop, straight past their house and down the main street. At last it crashed into a man who was running out of the jeweller's shop. He tripped over it and fell down.

'Oh no!' cried Huey, Dewey and Louie together. Then they saw that the bag the man had been carrying had opened and the contents were scattered all over the ground. The boys gasped with surprise! There were lots of sparkling jewels. The runaway hoop had knocked over a jewel thief!

The boys raced down the hill and grabbed the stunned robber just as the jeweller came rushing out of his shop. His worried expression changed to delight. 'Well done, boys,' he said. 'How clever of you to use your hoop like that! I think you deserve a reward!' And with that he took out his wallet and pulled out three five-pound notes.

Just at that moment, Donald came puffing up. 'It's my hoop actually,' he said smiling, and before the surprised jeweller could protest, he pocketed the reward money and made off down the street.

Huey, Dewey and Louie were most upset. They hurried down the street after Donald, just in time to see him going into the toy shop!

'Maybe he's buying us another present,' said Dewey, hopefully, as they peered through the window.

'No such luck,' groaned Louie. 'Just look at him!'

The triplets gazed in amazement as they saw Uncle Donald testing out a pair of roller skates across the toy shop floor. Disgusted, they decided to go home.

As they walked along the road, they heard Uncle Donald behind them.

'Wait for me, boys!' he shouted, waving his arms and skating along the pavement.

Huey, Louie and Dewey turned round and said together, 'No we won't,' and they all three ran home as fast as they could. They decided that in future, Uncle Donald could be left to get into trouble on his own!

Mickey Mouse at the Fair

Mickey Mouse was curled up in his favourite armchair, reading the paper. When he got to the horoscope page, he read his own horoscope aloud. It said, 'Beware of sudden shocks caused by surprise visitors.'

'Well, I won't have to worry about that,' Mickey said to Pluto. 'I'm going to be out all day as we are taking Morty and Ferdie to the funfair today.'

Later that morning, Mickey, Pluto, Morty and Ferdie climbed into Mickey's car and drove off to the funfair. As soon as they arrived, the twins leapt out of the car and rushed off to the dodgems. When it was their turn, they climbed into a nice pink and yellow car, and Pluto dived in between them.

'Come on Uncle Mickey,' shouted Morty. 'There's plenty of room.'

But Mickey shook his head. 'I'll stay here and watch,' he said.

The cars started off. Morty was steering and he had great fun trying to drive round without banging into any other cars. But at the end of their turn, they had had quite a few crashes and were feeling rather bruised.

Next, the boys wanted to go on the moon rockets. There was only room for the two of them so Mickey and Pluto waited for them on the ground. Mickey was very pleased that he could not go on the rockets but Pluto was bored.

The next ride was on the big dipper. Mickey heard the passengers screaming as they zoomed up and down along the track so he decided to stay on the ground again. But Morty, Ferdie and

Pluto clambered aboard eagerly.

At first, they moved slowly, but then the train gathered speed. They climbed up to the top and then seemed to fall away into space as they sped down again towards a bend. It looked as if they would go off the edge but at the last moment, they turned the corner and the train started to climb up another steep bit.

Morty and Ferdie loved every minute and they laughed and screamed like everyone else. But Pluto was really scared. His ears stood up on end and he was so frightened he couldn't even howl. Mickey was quite sure he had made the right decision to stay with his feet firmly on the ground.

At last the ride was over and Morty and Ferdie scrambled out of their car, followed by a very shaken Pluto!

'We're hungry,' said the boys when Mickey met them.

The excitement of the ride had given them an appetite so Mickey bought all of them a hot dog.

'What shall we do now?' asked Ferdie when he had finished eating.

'Let's go to the Hall of Mirrors,' suggested Morty, and he set off towards the entrance.

Inside, they all laughed at each other in the different mirrors. Mickey looked tall and thin in one mirror, then he looked short and fat in another. They saw Pluto upside down and Morty found a mirror in which he looked bent in the middle. Ferdie saw himself shaped like an S.

Before long, Pluto got bored with the Hall of Mirrors and he ran off to visit the next ride – the Ghost Train.

'Come back, Pluto!' called Mickey.

But Pluto ran on, and soon he disappeared into a tunnel, wagging his tail.

'Oh well,' said Mickey. 'We'll have to follow him I suppose,' and he paid for three tickets. 'At least this ride is firmly on the ground!'

So Morty, Ferdie and Mickey climbed into one of the carriages and entered the Ghost Train in search of Pluto.

'Aaahh!' screamed Morty and Ferdie as ghosts sprang out of cupboards and spiders dropped down from the ceiling. They weren't really frightened, just excited. But Mickey was too scared to utter a sound. It was very dark but lights flashed on and off showing skeletons and huge hands. Once, they saw a skull with green flashing eyes.

Suddenly, a sign lit up in front of them: 'Beware – the Hound of the Baskervilles', and a large snarling beast leapt out of the shadows. Even Morty and Ferdie jumped. A second later, another snarling beast leapt right into their carriage, and landed on Mickey's lap. His heart nearly stopped, and he suddenly remembered what his horoscope had said. Surprise visitors! Sudden shocks! This must be it.

Terrified, Mickey clung to his seat, hardly daring to breathe. The beast that had landed on his lap felt very real. Then the train burst through the doors back into the sunshine and Mickey saw that the snarling beast on his lap was none other than Pluto!

Pluto thought he'd been very clever fooling the others. He had wanted to get his own back on them after he had been so frightened on the big dipper. Morty and Ferdie laughed when they saw Pluto and congratulated him on his joke.

When Mickey had recovered he saw the funny side too. 'Come on, I'll buy you some candyfloss,' he said, laughing, 'as long as I don't have to go on any more rides!'

Donald Duck and the Witch

It was nearly Halloween, and Donald Duck and his nephews had been looking for pumpkins to make lanterns out of. It was late and getting dark by the time they had found four suitable ones. As they walked home, each holding a big round pumpkin, Huey suddenly shouted, 'Look! A witch on a broomstick.'

They all saw something streak across the sky.

'Pooh!' said Donald. 'Witches, pooh! There are no witches, you know that. It must have been some sort of bird you saw.'

But the boys knew that it had been a real witch they had seen, so the next day they went to look for her. They walked for a long time through the woods, and as there was no path to follow they were not at all sure where they were going. At last they heard a

cackle not far away. Immediately they knew they had found the witch, as who else could laugh like that?

'Sh!' said Dewey, putting his finger to his lips, and he started to find a way through the undergrowth. They came out in a clearing where they soon saw the witch's house. Smoke rose from the chimney and steam rolled up in clouds from a cauldron in the front.

'Welcome, boys, welcome,' said the witch's voice. 'Welcome to Witch Hazel's little home.' Then they saw her hobbling towards them, cackling and grinning.

The boys were amazed.

'What can I do for you today?' Witch Hazel asked them. 'Any spells you'd like me to cast? Anybody you'd like me to bewitch?' She poked Louie in the ribs with her elbow and winked at him.

'Bewitch Uncle Donald,' they cried. Then they told Witch Hazel how Donald didn't believe in witches.

'We'll show him!' she cackled, beckoning them close. She took some mysterious things out of her pockets and threw them into her cauldron. Smoke swirled up in odd shapes and the boys could smell a peculiar smell.

'We'll show that Donald,' promised Witch Hazel as she stirred the cauldron. 'Be sure to come and meet me here on Halloween.'

Huey, Dewey and Louie went home very excited, but they did not tell Donald anything about their adventure.

On Halloween, the boys disappeared early and Donald was not surprised when his doorbell rang later that evening. He opened the door and there stood three witches. He easily recognized his three nephews through their disguises and he laughed to himself as he opened the door wide. In came the witches, one, two, three – four!

Now Donald was surprised. He didn't expect four witches. They all had broomsticks which they left by the door. Donald thought he saw one of the broomsticks move, but that was impossible. The light must be playing tricks on him. He tried not to show any concern as the four witches sat down.

Donald didn't wait for one of his nephews to say, 'Trick or treat!' He would rather give them a gift than be a victim of one of their tricks. But he had some tricks of his own. 'Have a treat,' he said as he handed round a plate of little cakes.

'Ouch!' cried Dewey when he picked up a cake. There was a mouse trap stuck on his thumb.

'Wow!' cried Louie who took one next. His was a jack-in-the-box.

'Glub!' gulped Huey. When he bit into his, he discovered it was made of rubber.

'Thanks,' said the fourth witch. Then with a cackle she blew her cake and it exploded into dust right in Donald's face.

'Serves you right,' said a voice behind him. Donald whirled round but there were only some pumpkin-lanterns sitting there, grinning. As he looked he was sure he saw one of the faces laughing at him.

'We must be going now,' said one of the witches. 'Come with us and we'll return your hospitality.'

'No thanks,' said Donald, but he had no choice. He tried to cling on to the door handle but could not help being swept out of the house, and he soon found himself riding a broomstick.

'Abracadabra, boys! Here we go!' a voice cackled. Then to Donald's horror he saw the ground falling away. He was flying. Up above the trees he went and seemed to be heading straight for the Moon. But then he was suddenly falling down into the woods.

'Welcome to Witch Hazel's home,' he heard a witch say, then he tumbled straight into a cauldron while the other three witches roared with laughter. He choked and spluttered in the cauldron and when at last he was hauled out, he was soaking wet and very angry. The witches did not notice, though, as they could hardly stand up, they were laughing so much.

Witch Hazel fetched some dry clothes for Donald and when he came out of the house, he saw a huge table covered with a Halloween feast. There was pumpkin pie, apple pie, corn on the cob and all sorts of delicious things.

'Have a real treat Uncle Donald,' his nephews said as they took off their masks. Then they all sat down to eat.

It didn't take long for Donald to manage a smile. 'I still don't believe in witches,' he said to Witch Hazel, 'but if there were any, I'd want them all to be like you!'

Mickey Mouse's Picnic

Mickey Mouse was feeling very happy. He was going for a picnic with his friends and it was a beautiful day. He sang a song as he skipped up the path to Minnie's house:

'What a beautiful day for a picnic,
What a picnical day for a lark!
We will frolic all day
In the happiest way,
And we won't get back home until dark.'

'Ready Minnie?' he called when he reached her front door.

'Ready!' said Minnie.

Mickey peeked inside the picnic basket. Minnie had packed huge peanut butter and jam sandwiches, cold meat sandwiches, devilled eggs, potato salad, radishes, onions, fizzy pink lemonade and a great big chocolate cake.

'Let's go!' said Mickey, and he picked up the basket and led Minnie out to the car. Pluto, Goofy, Daisy Duck and Clarabelle Cow were waiting.

'It seems strange to go on a picnic without Donald Duck,' said Mickey as they drove away.

'Yes, but there is always trouble when Donald comes,' said the others.

Everyone sang as they drove along.

'What a beautiful day for a picnic,
What a picnical day for a lark!'

None of them saw a figure come out from behind a bush when the car had passed. It jumped up and down with rage. It was Donald Duck.

It started out to be a perfect day. First they looked for a good picnic spot beside the river and they found the perfect place beneath a tall shady tree. They left their things there including the picnic basket and everyone jumped into the river for a swim. The water

was cool and fresh and the friends swam, dived, played games and had a wonderful time.

'I'm hungry enough to eat that whole basketful of lunch myself,' said Mickey after a while.

We'll see that you don't, Mickey!' Minnie laughed. 'But it is time to eat now, I think.'

They all scrambled out of the water and hurried off to dress.

'Look at this!' Goofy cried, as he held up his trousers. The legs were tied into knots. So were his shirt sleeves, and Mickey's were too.

'Well I never!' said Clarabelle Cow.

'Some mischief-maker must be around,' Mickey said, with a shake of his head. But Minnie thought of something else. 'The lunch!' she cried, and she rushed to the big old tree. The picnic basket had gone.

'Oh no!' groaned everyone. 'Not the lunch!'

'Hurry and get dressed everyone,' Mickey cried. 'We'll soon find out about this.'

They struggled to undo the knots in their clothes, and set off to search for their lunch. They hunted everywhere but found no sign of the picnic basket. At last they came to Mickey's car. They were hot and tired and hungry and cross.

It was then that they met Donald Duck. He was walking along the road with a fishing rod over one shoulder and a bundle hanging from the end of it.

He was whistling as he walked along, and he looked very pleased with himself. 'Well, hello, hello, hello!' he cried. 'Imagine meeting all of you out here. I've just come from doing some fishing. I got tired of spending a lonely day at home.'

'Oh-er-yes,' said Mickey. He felt a bit guilty because they had not asked Donald to come on their picnic.

'Where are you going?' Donald asked.

'We are hunting for our lunch,' Mickey said.

'For lunch?' said Donald. 'Why I've enough for us all in my bundle here. I will happily share it with my friends.'

Now everyone felt guilty but they were so hungry that they thanked Donald very much. They all sat down under the same shady tree, and Donald opened his bundle.

The lunch was delicious. There were peanut butter and jam sandwiches, cold meat sandwiches, devilled eggs, potato salad, radishes, onions, pink lemonade and a great big chocolate cake! Minnie and Mickey Mouse looked a bit surprised when they saw that picnic lunch, but they didn't say a word.

Everyone ate and ate until they could not eat any more.

'This is delicious, Donald,' said Clarabelle Cow.

'And it is nice of you, too, Donald,' Daisy Duck added, 'to share it with us.'

'Sure is,' said Goofy, and he began eating yet another sandwich.

'Yes,' Mickey admitted. 'I think we misjudged you, Donald, old boy.'

'Humph!' said Minnie Mouse. She turned to Donald. 'Did you bring a knife for cutting the chocolate cake, Donald?' she asked.

'Er-ah, I had one somewhere,' Donald said, but he couldn't find it anywhere.

'I fastened a knife to the bottom of *my* cake plate with sticky tape,' Minnie told them all.

Mickey picked up the cake on its plate and looked at the bottom. There, sure enough, was a knife fastened to the bottom of the plate. On the handle were the letters MM.

'Well!' said Minnie.

'Why, Donald,' cried Daisy Duck.

'So that's where our lunch disappeared to,' cried Mickey Mouse.

Donald looked down at the ground. 'I'm sorry, really I am,' he said. 'I won't ever do it again.' He was very ashamed.

'Where is my picnic basket?' Minnie asked.

'In Mickey's car,' Donald admitted.

Mickey began to laugh. 'Well,' he said, 'you know you should not take people's picnics, Donald, but I think you've learned your lesson. And so have we. We should have invited you to come on our picnic.'

Everyone agreed then, and when they had finished their lunch and cleared everything away, they all piled back into Mickey's car. They made room for Donald to sit in the empty picnic basket, and away they went towards town, singing:

'We will frolic all day
In the happiest way,
And we won't get back home until
dark!'

Doc Swaller and the Green-Spot Cure

One cold winter's day, Huey, Dewey and Louie woke up with a sick feeling – watery eyes, sniffly noses, ruffled feathers, chills and some reddish spots on their yellow beaks.

'I don't feel well,' moaned Huey.

'Me neither,' groaned Dewey.

Louie sneezed. 'I know what this means,' he said gloomily. 'It means that we can't go to school.'

Just then, Grandma walked into the room. 'Oh goodness!' she exclaimed. 'This looks like the worst case of Duckburg McMeasles I've ever seen. You and your spots will have to stay at home today.'

'Oh Grandma,' Louie said. 'Isn't there anything that will get rid of these spots in a hurry? I shall get so bored in bed all day.'

'I'm afraid not,' Grandma answered. 'You've got the real McMeasles all right. But did I ever tell you about old Doc Swaller and the mysterious green-spot epidemic?'

The boys just looked watery-eyed and shook their heads. They loved to hear Grandma's stories of long ago. So Grandma began . . .

It was the first fine day of spring at Duckfoot Crossing. The snow had finally melted, the air smelt fresh and flowery and the children skipped and sang all the way to school. They played in the playground enjoying the warm spring weather.

Suddenly Miss Pinkerton appeared at the door of the school, ringing her big brass bell. The boys and girls obediently marched inside, but they kept looking back through the doorway. All through the winter they had enjoyed being inside, but now all they could think about was sunshine and green grass.

Of course, at lunch time, all the children rushed outside. Little Bo Dilly had a sly grin on his face as he skipped into the playground. 'Hey, everybody! Gather round. I have a great idea,' he yelled.

Everyone came running. When Bo had an idea, it was always a great idea, and they all wanted to hear. In a large huddle, with heads bent, they all listened to Bo's plan. Then, one by one, heads popped up. The children were smiling, giggling and even laughing out loud. And before long, they all disappeared into the woods near by, where they often went to collect leaves, rocks and flowers.

Soon Miss Pinkerton rang the bell to signal the end of the break. She was thinking how empty the playground looked when Bo appeared. He hobbled past her looking rather ill. To her amazement she noticed that his arms and face were covered with green spots. A second child walked through

the door. Her face and arms were also covered with green spots. Then a third came in, and a fourth, until one by one the entire class filed in, all spotted with green.

'Grumbling grasshoppers,' groaned the schoolteacher.

'We don't feel very well, Miss,' complained a voice in the corner. 'We must have picked up a rash in the woods.'

'I suppose we'll all have to go home,' suggested Bo, with a touch of that sly grin still on his face.

'You're not going anywhere until I get Doc Swaller over here to take a look at all of you,' Miss Pinkerton announced. The green-spotted creatures looked at one another. Things weren't going as Bo had planned!

Miss Pinkerton rang up Doc Swaller and explained the situation.

'It sounds serious,' he said. 'I'll be over right away.'

In a short time the old doctor arrived with his big black bag. Suddenly everyone was very quiet. He listened to heartbeats and looked at tongues. He thumped at knees and chests. He looked into eyes, ears and mouths. 'Hmmmmm,' he said. 'Very interesting.'

'We'll just have to rest at home and get lots of fresh air and sunshine. Right Doc?' said Bo.

'I'm afraid not, son,' said Doc Swaller. 'This is serious. It looks to me like a severe case of green-spotted fever. There's only one sure cure that I know of.' He rummaged through his bag and pulled out some bottles and jars, a big glass bowl, and a spoon. Whistling softly, he began mixing things in the bowl.

The children watched. Strange things happened! The stuff in the bowl made bubbling, squeaking noises. It turned orange, then red, then purple. Then the bubbling stopped. The bowl was filled with purple goo!

'There,' said Doc Swaller.

'Is that the cure?' the children gasped.

'The only cure there is,' smiled Doc Swaller. 'Just rub it on your spots every day and stay out of the sun for a week.'

Suddenly Bo said, 'Oh, gosh, am I thirsty! May I please get a drink?' And before Miss Pinkerton could answer, Bo dashed out of the door. He filled a basin with water and then began splashing his face and arms. The spots began to disappear. When they were all gone Bo calmly strolled back into the classroom.

'Your spots are gone,' someone cried.

'So they are,' said Bo, trying to look as if he were surprised.

'I'm thirsty too!' 'Me too!' 'Me too!' the other children chimed in. And one by one they jumped up and ran outside. There was a frantic hubbub of splashing as everyone began washing. Soon they returned to the classroom – minus their spots.

'What a remarkable recovery,' Miss Pinkerton exclaimed. 'Isn't this amazing, Doc Swaller?'

'Just what I said,' proclaimed the wise doctor. 'It's the only cure there is.' Then with a wink of his eye and a wave of his hand, he left the children and Miss Pinkerton and whistled his way home in the warm spring sunshine.

* * *

When Grandma Duck had finished the story Louie said, 'Those children really got well quickly didn't they Grandma?'

'Yes,' Grandma replied as she tucked them in. 'And you will too. We'll start with some of Grandma's cure for spots – toast and my very own plum jam.'

Pluto's Bone

Pluto was enjoying himself. He had a big meaty bone and was happily chewing it in Mickey's garden. But the bone was so big that he couldn't finish it. He looked around for a good place to hide it. He could finish it tomorrow. He decided that one of Mickey's flowerbeds would be just the place.

So Pluto picked up the bone in his mouth and walked over to a suitable flowerbed. With his front paws he began to dig a hole in the soft earth. It had to be quite a big hole as it was a big bone.

When he had almost finished digging, Mickey came out of his house. 'What are you doing Pluto?' he shouted. 'Bad dog. You're ruining my garden,' and he picked up a tulip that Pluto had dug out of the flowerbed. 'Go and bury your bone somewhere else,' he said crossly.

Pluto was extremely upset. That flowerbed had been the perfect place for his bone.

But then Mickey had a better idea. 'I know,' he said. He took Pluto's bone and threw it in the dustbin, replacing the lid with a loud bang.

When Mickey had gone back indoors, Pluto sat down by the dustbin and stared at it. How on earth was he going to get his bone back? Then he heard a familiar sound. The dustmen were coming. Pluto was thrilled. Now he would get his bone back. He began to wag his tail.

The dustcart stopped outside the

house and a dustman came up the path. 'Hello, Pluto,' he said, and patted him on the head. Then he took the lid off the dustbin and lifted it on to his back. Pluto watched him walk back to the cart and waited for the right moment to take back his bone. The dustman put the bin down on the pavement for a second while some other dustmen emptied their bins into the cart.

Pluto saw his chance. He dived, head first, into the bin to get the bone, but it was the wrong thing to do. Before he had time to get out again, the dustman lifted up the bin and tipped the contents, with Pluto and his bone, into the cart. The cart moved off and Pluto was carried away in it under a pile of rubbish.

While they were driving along, Pluto wriggled free of all the rubbish. He found his bone and prepared to leap out at the first chance he got. But he didn't know that the next stop for the dustmen was by the river. At last the dustcart came to a stop and the door opened. Immediately Pluto leapt out – and plunged straight into the river.

The dustmen couldn't think how Pluto had got into the cart but they rushed to save him. One of them held on to his back legs and dragged him out of the water. Poor Pluto watched as his bone sank to the bottom of the river, leaving just a few bubbles on the surface.

Unhappily, Pluto trudged home, boneless. He'd had an awful day and he felt very sorry for himself. He'd been scolded by Mickey, buried in a pile of rubbish, shut in a dustcart and had then fallen in the river. And the worst thing of all was he'd lost his bone. He flopped down on the pavement and howled.

Meanwhile, Mickey had begun to feel guilty about throwing Pluto's bone away. He went out and bought him another one. It was a large meaty one, even better than the first one.

On the way out of the butcher's shop, he saw a group of people standing round, looking at something on the pavement. Whatever it was was making a terrible noise. Mickey stopped to have a look and blushed. It was Pluto!

'Poor thing,' said someone. 'He's starving. He probably hasn't had anything to eat for days.'

Then someone else saw Mickey. 'That dog belongs to you doesn't he? You mean thing. Give him that bone.' She snatched the bone out of Mickey's hands and gave it to Pluto.

At last Pluto was happy. He ran all the way home with his new bone firmly in his mouth. And he knew exactly how to get another one!

Donald Duck and the Christmas Carol

'Deck the halls with boughs of holly!' sang Donald Duck and his nephews. It was Christmas Eve. They had done all their Christmas shopping and were now decorating their Christmas tree. They were admiring the tree when the doorbell rang. Huey, Louie and Dewey ran to open the door. 'Merry Christmas! Merry Christmas!' they cried.

'Bah!' said Uncle Scrooge who was standing on the doorstep. He shook the snow from his coat as he stamped into the house. 'Christmas? Humbug!'

'Christmas, humbug? Why, Uncle Scrooge! How can you say such a thing?' cried Huey, Louie and Dewey.

'Christmas is a waste of time and money,' snapped Uncle Scrooge. I came to see if Donald would drive me out to my farm to bury these sacks of money I've saved up this year. I'll bet you haven't got any money saved after buying all these stupid presents. And I can see you're determined to waste your time, too. So – Bah! Humbug! And goodbye to you.' Uncle Scrooge stormed out of the house, carrying his money sacks, and he struggled off into the snow.

'Wait, Uncle Scrooge!' called Huey, Louie, and Dewey.

But Uncle Scrooge wouldn't wait. He just grunted and shook his cane at all the Christmas shoppers.

'Old skinflint!' cried Donald. 'Trying to spoil our Christmas just because he won't have one of his own.'

'Poor Uncle Scrooge! No Christmas at all! What will he do Uncle Donald?' asked the boys.

'He'll go home and lock the door and draw the curtains and sit all alone in his dark, cold house, feeling sorry for himself,' said Donald Duck.

'He will?' said the boys. 'Well why don't we . . . ' and after whispering to each other they continued to decorate their Christmas tree.

Donald had been right. Uncle Scrooge went home to his large, old, empty house, grumbling all the way. He locked the door and drew all the curtains, shutting out all signs and sounds of Christmas. In the evening, he went upstairs to his cold, dark bedroom and climbed into his four-poster bed. Propping himself up on his pillows he began to read his book. 'Christmas – humbug,' he muttered to himself. 'I don't care for anyone, and nobody cares for me. That's the way, if I had my say, that everyone would be.'

The candle sputtered and shadows danced on the walls. Uncle Scrooge began to doze. His head dropped over the book and he was almost asleep when he heard a knock on his door. In came a figure dressed all in white, with a holly wreath on its head. In its hands it carried a big black book.

'Who – who are you?' asked Uncle Scrooge.

'I am the ghost of Christmas Past,' said the figure. 'Do you remember the fun you used to have at Christmastime?' And putting the big book into Scrooge's hands, the figure slipped out of the door.

Uncle Scrooge looked at the book. It was an old photograph album. 'Why, there's Daisy,' he cried, 'with the doll I gave her one year. And little Donald on his rocking horse. My, what fun we used to have!'

Uncle Scrooge was so busy looking at the photographs that he did not notice the door open again. A second figure, dressed all in red, slipped into the room. 'I am the spirit of Christmas Present,' it said. 'Listen to the fun others are having this Christmas.'

Outside his door, Scrooge could hear happy voices singing,

'Deck the halls with boughs of holly,
Fa la la la la la la la la.
'Tis the season to be merry,
Fa la la la la la la la la.'

'Bah . . .' Uncle Scrooge began, but he was starting to feel a bit lonely.

Then a third figure came into the room. This one was dressed all in black. 'I am the spirit of Christmas Yet to Come,' it said. 'If you do not mend your ways, you will never have a happy Christmas again.'

'But what can I do?' cried Uncle Scrooge.

'Follow me!' said the figure, and it went out of the room.

Uncle Scrooge jumped out of bed and followed the figure along the dark corridor and down the stairs. They went towards the living-room.

'There's nothing in there but dust,' said Uncle Scrooge. Nevertheless, he followed the figure into the room.

'Merry Christmas, Uncle Scrooge!' Daisy and Donald and Huey, Louie and Dewey were all in the room.

A beautiful Christmas tree stood in the corner of the room and round it was heaped the biggest pile of presents Uncle Scrooge had ever seen. Some of them were for him! Of course he was thrilled and he couldn't speak, he was so surprised. He decided he liked Christmas after all! At last he said, 'Let's take my sacks of money this morning and give some to everyone we see who doesn't look as if they're having as merry a Christmas as we are. For always remember this, boys,' he said, 'Christmas is the best day of all!'

Donald the Explorer

It was snowing. Donald Duck was indoors reading. His book was about an explorer who had been to the South Pole.

There were three or four pictures of penguins in the book. Donald liked to look at these pictures. 'I'd like to see some penguins,' said Donald to himself. 'This book says they are very hard to catch.

'The explorer didn't bring any back with him. He caught some but they got away. When I go to the South Pole, I shall bring back a lot of penguins. They won't get away from me.'

Donald turned the page and went on reading. The more he read, the more he wanted to go to the South Pole.

After a while, he looked out of the window. He was surprised to see Goofy coming slowly through the deep snow. He was walking on skis and was dragging a sledge. The sledge was piled high with all kinds of bundles and packages.

Donald pulled on his sweater and grabbed his scarf and hat. Then he ran out to meet Goofy. 'Hi, Goofy,' he said. 'Where are you going, dragging all that stuff with you?'

'I'm going to the South Pole,' said Goofy, 'I hear it's a wonderful place. I have blankets and food and other things on my sledge.'

'Will you let me come too?' asked Donald.

'Of course,' said Goofy, 'if you help pull the sledge.'

Donald ran quickly into the house. In a short time he came back carrying a butterfly net, a large bird cage, and a

package. He put these on Goofy's sledge with the other things.

'What are you going to do with those things, Donald?' asked Goofy.

'I shall catch some young penguins with the net,' said Donald, 'and I'll bring them back in the cage.'

'What's in the package?' asked Goofy.

'A black coat and a white shirt,' said Donald. 'I'm going to wear them. That ought to fool the penguins. They'll think I'm another penguin when they see me all black and white.'

'They say penguins are very intelligent,' said Goofy.

'Well, even if they are, I'm going to catch one,' said Donald. 'They aren't any more intelligent than me.'

The two of them started off on their journey. Goofy pulled the sledge and Donald pushed, and after some time they reached the South Pole.

They made a hole in the ice and caught some fish for supper. Then Goofy suggested that they make an igloo to live in.

'You start the igloo,' said Donald. 'I'm going to catch a penguin.' He dressed himself up in the black coat and white shirt and he really did look a bit like a penguin! Then he tied a fish on a string to a short pole. This was supposed to be bait for catching penguins. He carried the butterfly net and the bird cage and set off.

Donald walked along for some time. At last he saw something small and black in the snow. He put down the bird cage and walked towards the black thing. It was a baby penguin. It stood and stared at Donald instead of running away.

Donald held out the stick so that the fish on the end hung right in front of the little penguin's beak. But the penguin did not try to eat it. Instead, it suddenly grew frightened and turned and hurried away. Donald followed and tried to get the butterfly net over the baby penguin's head. But the little penguin was too quick.

In no time at all, penguins rushed at Donald from all sides. There were big penguins, little penguins and middle-sized penguins. Two of the biggest ones took hold of Donald, one on each side, as though they were policemen.

Donald tried to tell them that he did not mean to hurt the little penguin. But the penguins did not understand him and he could not understand them. He was, however, quite sure that they were very angry.

The biggest penguin of all came up to Donald, carrying Donald's bird cage.

He opened the door of the cage and pushed Donald in, shutting the door behind him.

Donald was very frightened. The penguins walked all round him, making fun of him. He was sure that they were laughing at him. After a while, they all gathered in a huddle and talked together. They were obviously planning what to do with him.

Suddenly, Donald thought of Goofy. Perhaps Goofy could scare away the penguins. He began to shout and pound on the cage, hoping that Goofy would hear him. But Goofy did not come and Donald at last stopped shouting. It was no use.

The penguins came out of their huddle and waddled away to a small hill. There they began to slide down the hill on flat pieces of ice. They seemed to be having a great deal of fun.

Donald knew he could open the cage door if only he had a chance. He hoped that the penguins would take their eyes off him. Then, when they seemed very busy sliding, he unfastened the door, but held it closed, waiting for the right time to escape.

Just then, one penguin crashed into another one. Others bumped into them and there was quite a pile up. The penguins did not seem to be watching the cage then, so Donald took the chance. He took off his black coat and hung it on one side of the cage. Then he quickly pushed the door open and crawled out. He hoped the penguins

would see the black coat and think he was still in the cage. He still had on the white shirt and this would help him hide from them as he crawled along in the snow.

Donald needn't have bothered. The penguins had thought it was a good joke to scare him, but now they were enjoying sliding down the hill. They had lost interest in Donald. Penguins are like that!

Donald crawled along in the snow until he bumped into Goofy who was out looking for him.

'Hurry up Donald!' said Goofy. 'What are you doing? The fish are so well cooked, they are all dried up.'

'I've had a terrible time, Goofy!' said Donald.

'Oh dear. Come inside and tell me about it,' said Goofy kindly. 'Did you see any penguins?'

'Yes I did,' said Donald, 'and I don't want to see another one as long as I live. Never, never, NEVER! I don't like the South Pole anyway. Why did you bring me here?'

'Well we don't have to stay,' said the good-natured Goofy. 'We'll go back in the morning.'

So they went home the next day, and that was the end of the famous Goofy-Donald Polar Expedition!

The Roaring Smoking Whiz-bang

Dale saw Grandma Duck, Daisy and everyone else come into the woods, but they didn't see him. He heard them talking, but they didn't hear him because he wasn't talking to anyone. Chip was taking a nap.

Daisy spread a blanket on the grass. 'Ah,' she said, sitting down. 'There's nothing like the cool of the woods on a warm summer's day. We will be able to have a lovely picnic.'

Huey, Dewey and Louie put their baskets on the grass. 'Let's eat now,' said Huey.

'Why wait?' asked Dewey.

'Eating is the best part of a picnic,' said Louie.

'No eating,' said Grandma, 'until our guest of honour arrives. Today is his birthday, after all.'

'Do you think he'll come on the whiz-bang?' asked Huey.

Daisy shuddered. 'I suppose he will,' she said, 'and I suppose it'll be roaring and smoking as usual.'

Dale was listening to all this. He imagined what a roaring, smoking whiz-bang looked like and he didn't like it one bit. He shivered and scampered away to wake up Chip.

'Chip, wake up,' he whispered when he found him. 'A roaring, smoking whiz-bang is coming this way.'

Chip half-opened one sleepy eye. 'Tell me when it gets here,' he said.

'But Chip,' wailed Dale, 'what will happen?'

'Mmm,' sighed Chip. He turned over and settled down more comfortably.

Dale imagined what the whiz-bang might do. Anything that roared would probably eat everything in sight. Anything that smoked would turn the woods into a barbecue. And Chip wouldn't wake up! He took a deep breath. 'I will be brave,' he promised himself, and he ran back to the picnic to find out more about the whiz-bang.

Huey, Dewey and Louis were playing a game, but Daisy was still talking to Grandma. 'It's so dangerous,' she said.

'It looks dangerous,' said Grandma, 'but Donald likes it.'

'When he roars in and skids to a stop,' said Daisy, 'it raises enough dust to blot out the Sun.'

Dale shuddered. The roaring, smoking whiz-bang sounded worse and worse. He dashed back to Chip. 'Ch-Ch-Chip,' he said, his teeth chattering. 'That roaring, smoking whiz-bang blots out the Sun.'

'Wake me up . . . zz-zz-zz . . . when it comes . . . zz-zz-zz,' murmured Chip, and he went back to sleep.

Dale hopped up and down anxiously. What was he going to do? The birds would have no light to hunt for seeds. The grasshoppers would bump into each other in the dark. He and Chip wouldn't be able to find their storehouse of hazelnuts. What would happen to the birds and the grasshoppers and Chip 'n' Dale? He covered Chip with leaves so that the whiz-bang wouldn't see him.

When Dale ran back to the picnic, Huey, Dewey and Louie were talking.

'That whiz-bang is so red,' said Huey, 'it practically glows in the dark.'

'It moves fast,' said Dewey. 'I bet it travels a million miles a minute.'

Dale groaned and gnawed at his knuckles. He and Chip couldn't run that fast. Then he heard something. It came from far away. 'Va-roooom!' Was it thunder? The noise grew louder. 'Va-rooooom!' No it wasn't thunder.

Dale turned and ran. 'Help!' he squeaked. 'It's coming. The red, glow-in-the-dark, roaring, smoking whiz-bang is coming!' He streaked through the woods and stumbled over Chip.

Chip sat up from his nap, and leaves flew all around him. 'What's going on?' he asked.

Dale jumped up and down. 'It's here,' he stuttered. 'The roaring, smoking whiz-bang is here. What are we going to do?'

Chip yawned, stretched and stood up. 'I've never heard of a roaring, smoking whiz-bang,' he said.

It'll eat up everything it sees,' said Dale. 'It'll turn the woods into a giant barbecue. It blots out the Sun. It glows in the dark. It runs a million miles a minute, and we can't run that fast,' he wailed.

A noise shattered the stillness. 'VA-ROOOOM!'

'And it's here now,' moaned Dale.

'I've got to see this,' said Chip, and he trotted through the woods towards

the noise, followed by Dale. They got to the picnic spot just in time.

'VA-ROOOOM . . . va-rooom . . . varooom. Bang! Bang!' When the noise died down, Chip peeked out from behind a tree and Dale peeked out from behind Chip. The smoke faded in the air, the dust settled to the ground, and Donald climbed down off the roaring, smoking whiz-bang.

'Happy Birthday, Donald,' shouted Grandma and Daisy and Huey and Dewey, and Louie.

'Oh thank you,' said Donald 'I never expected you to remember. Is that why you asked me to meet you here?'

While Donald and Grandma, Daisy, Huey, Dewey and Louie ate sandwiches and birthday cake, Chip tiptoed over to the whiz-bang. 'It's the reddest thing

I've ever seen,' he said. 'You're right. It roars, it smokes and it definitely raises dust, but it's only a big red motorcycle.'

Dale reached out and put a paw on the whiz-bang. The birds and the grasshoppers and Chip and he were safe. He let out a huge sigh of relief. And then, while Donald gave rides to Huey, Dewey and Louie, Chip 'n' Dale had a picnic too. It was almost as good as hazelnuts.

The Toy Sailing Boat

'There,' said Donald Duck. 'At last it's finished!' He stood back to look at his toy sailing boat. Making it had been a big job. It had taken him all summer. But now the boat was finished and it was beautiful.

Donald put it on the mantelpiece. It was just the right place for it. The whole room looked better with the boat there.

'Building boats is very hungry work,' Donald said to himself, and he made himself a large lunch.

After lunch, he decided to try the boat out on the lake. But his hard work had made him sleepy so he settled down for a nap first.

Now, outside Donald's cottage, there was an old elm tree where two little chipmunks called Chip 'n' Dale lived. They had had no lunch at all.

'I'm hungry,' said Chip, as he rubbed his empty stomach.

'Me too,' said little Dale. But suddenly he cheered up. 'Look!' he said.

Chip looked and looked. At last he saw it – one lonely acorn still hanging to the branch of an oak tree down beside the lake. Down the elm tree the two chipmunks raced, across to the oak and up its rough-barked trunk.

'Mine,' cried Chip, reaching for the nut.

'I saw it first!' Dale cried.

So they pushed and they tugged and they tussled, until the acorn slipped through their fingers and fell, splash, into the lake.

The two little chipmunks looked so sad as they watched the acorn float away. But Dale had seen something else. 'Look!' he cried.

Chip looked. On a little island out in the middle of the lake stood a great big oak tree, weighed down with acorns on every side. Down to the shore the chipmunks ran, but the water was far too cold for them to swim across.

'How can we get to the acorns?' wondered Chip, as they walked back to their elm tree.

'I don't know,' said Dale. But he soon had an idea. 'Look in there!' he said, pointing through the window of Donald's cottage.

On the mantelpiece they could see the toy sailing boat. It was the perfect size for them and they realized they could sail to the oak tree in it.

'Come on,' said Dale, and they raced in through the cottage door. They had taken the boat down and were going out through the door when Donald stirred in his sleep. He soon woke up completely and remembered his boat. But suddenly, something outside the window caught his eye. It was his boat, out in the middle of the lake.

'I'll fix those chipmunks!' Donald said. He pulled out his fishing rod and reel and chose a painted fly. It looked just like a nut. 'This will do,' he said,

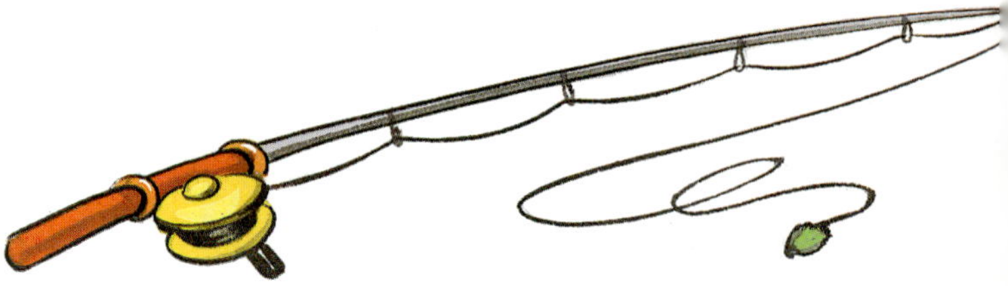

grinning, then he rushed to the lake and cast his fly right beside the sailing boat.

'Look! Here's a nut,' cried Dale. He picked up the floating fly. Then he tossed it into the hold.

As soon as the fly was caught fast in the hold, Donald pulled in the line. He pulled the little boat right into the shore. The chipmunks never noticed a thing. They did not even see Donald pouring water into the cabin of the

boat. Chip only discovered that when he went into the cabin. 'Man the pumps!' he cried.

Those two chipmunks worked with might and main to bale out the water while Donald watched and laughed. At last he couldn't help chuckling out loud and the chipmunks looked up.

'So that's the trouble!' Dale cried. He pulled out the fishing fly from the hold and flung it at Donald so that he was soon tangled up in fishing line.

Chip 'n' Dale set sail once more. Before Donald could launch his swift canoe, they had landed on the island in the middle of the lake. Quickly, they climbed the oak tree and began dancing on the branches. The oak tree seemed to shiver and shake as its store of acorns rained down. Chip and Dale were able to fill the little sailing boat with all the acorns they could possibly need.

Donald watched them from his canoe, while acorns fell all around him. 'Oh well,' he said. 'At least I know now that the boat will sail.'

When Chip 'n' Dale had brought their harvest to the shore, they stored the acorns in a hollow tree. Then they took Donald's toy boat and put it back exactly where they had found it.

Surprise, Surprise

'It's a good thing it's Daisy's birthday today,' said Huey. 'We only have to keep our surprise party secret from her for a few more hours.'

'Let's hurry up and make her birthday cake,' said Dewey. 'Then we can hide it.'

'That's the hardest part,' said Louie, who was trying to measure the flour. 'We've never made a cake without Daisy's help before.'

Just then, the doorbell rang. Louie ran to answer the door – and gulped. Daisy was standing there!

'My goodness, what are you doing in here?' asked Daisy when she went into the kitchen. 'It looks as though you could do with a little help.'

Huey, Dewey and Louie were speechless. They didn't want to tell her about the party. It would spoil the surprise. But they didn't want to lie, either. They had to think fast. Luckily they knew that Daisy had forgotten it was her birthday that day.

'Well Daisy, we're making a birthday cake,' said Huey.

'For a surprise party that we're giving for a friend,' said Dewey.

'And as you can see, we're not very good at making cakes,' Louie added.

'That's what I can do best,' said Daisy. 'I'll help you bake the cake. Then I can help you plan the rest of your party. Why don't you three start cleaning up the kitchen while I start measuring things.'

Huey, Dewey and Louie did a good job of cleaning up the kitchen and Daisy helped them make a birthday cake.

'Now,' said Daisy. 'What else do you have to do to get ready for the party?'

'Decorate the house,' said Huey.

'Make some party presents,' said Dewey.

'Plan some games,' said Louie.

'What about sending invitations?' asked Daisy.

'We don't have to send invitations,' said Louie, winking at Huey and Dewey. 'We went round from house to house and asked everyone to come to the party. But we could do with some help with putting up the decorations.'

Daisy helped Huey, Dewey and Louie all morning. By the time she had to go home, everything was ready for the party. The birthday cake was made and the house was decorated with balloons and streamers and ribbons and all kinds of colourful decorations. The table was set, there was a present for each guest and there were lots of games to play.

As Daisy prepared to go, Huey said to her, 'By the way, the party is at two o'clock. Why don't you come?'

'I'd love to,' said Daisy. 'See you then.'

On her way home, Daisy remembered that she should take a present for the person whose birthday it was. But she didn't know who it was.

She decided to buy a big, bouncy ball for the birthday person. That was something that anybody would like. So, she bought a blue and yellow ball, took it home and wrapped it up.

At two o'clock, sharp, Daisy rang the bell at Huey, Dewey and Louie's house. The house was very quiet, when Huey opened the door.

'Hello boys,' said Daisy looking round the empty room. 'Am I the first to arrive?'

Then suddenly, all of Daisy's friends jumped out from behind the sofa and the chairs and the door and shouted, 'Surprise!'

And Daisy was surprised. All she could say was, 'Oh my!'

Donald and Huey and Dewey and Louie and all of Daisy's friends sang,

'Happy birthday to you,
Happy birthday to you,
Happy birthday, dear Daisy,
Happy birthday to you.'

Everybody had a wonderful time because, of course, Daisy and the boys had planned it so well. At the end of the party Daisy hugged Huey, Dewey and Louie. 'Thank you all. It's the nicest surprise I've ever had,' she said. 'And next time you come over to my house you can play with the lovely present I gave myself!'

'We couldn't have done it without you,' said Huey, Dewey and Louie.

Mickey Mouse and Pluto Pup

Mickey Mouse woke up one sunny morning and decided to spend the day fishing with his dog, Pluto. He made Pluto's breakfast

in a big dog bowl, then he whistled for him from the back door. But Pluto did not appear.

Mickey looked everywhere for him until he noticed that the back gate was open. 'Aha! That's the answer,' he thought. 'I'll bet Pluto has gone to see Minnie,' and he jumped into his car and drove to Minnie's house.

'I'm looking for Pluto,' Mickey said when he met Minnie at her front door. 'Is he here?'

'Why, no,' said Minnie. 'I hope he's not lost. I'll help you look for him.'

So Mickey and Minnie jumped into the car and drove to Donald Duck's house. Donald was in the garden raking up leaves.

'We're looking for Pluto,' they told him. 'Is he here with you?'

'Why no,' said Donald. 'Is he lost? I'll help you look for him,' and he jumped into the car.

Just then, Donald's nephews, Huey, Dewey and Louie, came running up. 'Hey, Uncle Donald! Hey Uncle Mickey! Where are you going?' they cried.

'We're looking for Pluto,' Donald said.

'Can we come too?' the boys asked.

'Okay,' said Mickey.

So in they piled, and they all went over to Clarabelle Cow's house. Clarabelle Cow was out picking tomatoes. She waved when she saw them. 'Hello!' she called. 'How are you all?'

'Fine,' called the nephews. 'But we can't find Pluto.'

'Oh dear,' said Clarabelle. 'I'll help you look for him,' and she climbed into the car.

Soon they met Goofy.

'Gawsh,' said Goofy. 'Where are you folks all going to?'

'We're looking for Pluto,' Mickey called. 'Have you seen him?'

'Nope,' said Goofy, 'but I'll help you look for him.' So Goofy climbed into Mickey's car.

'Pluto might have gone to Horace Horse-collar's house,' suggested Minnie.

But Pluto had not gone to see Horace, so Horace came along to help look for him too.

Mickey's car was now packed full with all the friends and they set off to search for Pluto in the town. Mickey drove very slowly while everyone whistled and called for Pluto, but there was no sign of him.

'Wait!' cried the nephews suddenly. 'Stop here a minute Uncle Mickey. Listen!'

Mickey stopped the car and they all listened. From a big tent came the noise of all sorts of woofs and barks.

'The dog show!' cried Mickey. 'Of course! Why didn't we think of that?'

He quickly parked the car and hurried into the tent followed by all the others.

The dog show was nearly over. A blue rosette had been awarded to the best spaniel, the best terrier, the best poodle, the best work dog and the best hound. Now there was just one blue rosette left to be awarded. It was for the most popular dog in the show.

The dogs started marching past the judges' platform and who should come marching along with the rest but Pluto, holding his head very high.

'Pluto!' cried Mickey.

'There he is,' shouted Mickey's friends.

Pluto was very excited when he saw all his friends. He jumped about and turned somersaults. He rolled his eyes and flapped his ears and everyone at the dog show began to laugh and clap. They loved him and the judges were most impressed. Soon Pluto had a blue rosette too, for being the most popular dog in the show. He was very pleased with himself.

When it was all over, the friends piled back into Mickey's car, and Pluto sat proudly in the front seat. They drove back to Mickey's house where they celebrated Pluto's triumph with lots of ice cream and cake.

Donald Duck's Lucky Day

Huey, Dewey and Louie raced into the house. 'We're going to make lots of money this summer,' they said. 'We're going to take care of people's lawns.'

'Have you got a lawn mower?' asked Donald.

'Oh yes,' the three said together. 'It's a goat.'

'A goat,' exclaimed Donald. 'Goats can mean trouble. If I hear just one bad report about this goat, you'll have to get rid of it.'

All went well for several days. Then one evening, the boys asked Donald if they could have a party on the lawn. 'We'll pay for it ourselves,' they promised.

Donald agreed to the idea and the boys sent out the invitations to all their friends that evening.

Donald was reading his invitation the next afternoon when the phone rang. It was Daisy. 'Donald Duck,' she shouted down the phone. 'That goat has just eaten all my finest lilies. You'll have to get rid of it.' And she slammed down the receiver.

'Huey, Dewey, Louie,' Donald shouted, and the boys came running. 'Remember what I said about that goat? One bad report and it has to go. Well it's just eaten Aunt Daisy's best lilies. You have until Friday to get rid of it.'

Huey, Dewey and Louie huddled together. How could they get rid of the goat? They thought and thought until eventually, Dewey came up with an idea. He whispered it to the others.

On the day of the party, the boys met the guests at the gate.

'Here is your number for the grand prize,' said Dewey, slipping a card into each guest's hand.

After the races and games and ice cream and cake, Huey called for quiet. 'Now we'll draw for the grand prize,' he said. 'Watch your numbers.'

Dewey blindfolded Huey who then pulled a number out of a big box.

'Thirteen,' Dewey cried. 'The lucky number is thirteen.'

'That's my number,' quacked Donald Duck. 'I've got it!'

'Bring in the prize,' said Huey.

Then, from behind the shed came Louie. He was leading the prize – the boys' goat. Donald squawked with rage when he saw it. He was very angry.

'The goat is yours now,' said Huey.

'He doesn't belong to us any more,' said Louie.

'And it isn't Friday yet,' said Dewey.

Donald Duck-Mountain Climber

Huey, Dewey and Louie were sitting in front of the television, watching a programme about mountain climbing, while their uncle, Donald Duck, was reading.

'Uncle Donald,' they shouted. 'Look at those mountain climbers. They are really good. They could probably climb the highest mountain in the world.'

'If you think they're good,' said Donald, 'you should see me climb. Once upon a time I was the very best mountain climber anywhere.' He pointed to a photograph on the wall. 'Just look at that picture of me,' he continued. 'Whenever I went mountain climbing, I was always the first to reach the top.'

'I didn't know you were a mountain climber,' said Huey.

'Why don't you take us to some of those big mountains?' asked Dewey.

'It would be so much fun,' said Louie.

'You know,' said Donald. 'That sounds like a very good idea. I would like to do some mountain climbing again.'

So the very next day they all packed their bags and walked down to the station. Their friends Mickey and Minnie went to the station with them and so did Pluto.

'Have a good time,' shouted Mickey.

'And don't forget to be careful,' said Minnie, waving her pink handkerchief.

'Careful?' said Donald, as he climbed into the train. 'You're talking to an expert. I plan to show these boys a thing or two about the art of climbing mountains.'

All night long the train chugged along while Uncle Donald and his nephews slept. Then in the early morning, it travelled through a long dark mountain tunnel. When it came out the other end, into the bright sunshine, the boys woke up.

'Wow! Look at those mountains!' shouted Louie.

'Did you ever climb mountains like those?' Dewey asked his uncle.

Donald looked out of the window at the white snowy peaks. 'Of course I climbed mountains like those,' he said, 'and lots that were even higher than those.'

At last the train stopped at a little mountain village. Uncle Donald and his three nephews climbed off the train and, carrying their bags, walked down the main street. They stopped in front of the village inn.

'I'm Donald Duck, the mountain climber,' Uncle Donald told the innkeeper. 'Do you have room for me and my three nephews?'

'Indeed I do,' said the innkeeper. 'Let me show it to you.'

Huey, Dewey and Louie were very excited. They wanted to go climbing straight away. 'When can we get started, Uncle Donald?' they asked.

'Now just a minute,' said Uncle Donald. 'Mountain climbing is very dangerous. You will have time enough for that when you're older. The three of you can have a good time here at the inn while *I* am climbing.' Then, leaving his unhappy nephews at the inn, he went to look for a shop.

At last he stopped in front of a shop window filled with things for climbing. 'Wow!' he said. 'This is the place for me. I see everything I need.' And he opened the door and went in.

'Good morning, Mr Shopkeeper,' said Donald. 'I am Donald Duck the mountain climber.'

'You have come to just the right place, Mr Duck,' said the shopkeeper. 'I have everything you need, even a good guide. Goofy's my name, and I'm the best guide in the whole village.

'First you must have some good strong rope and some metal spikes,' said Goofy. 'Then you will want a hammer and a climbing ladder. And of course you have to have a back pack. Now, just follow your trusty guide,' he said, putting on his hat, and he set off towards the mountains.

Poor Donald could hardly walk under the load! Huey, Dewey and Louie came out to say goodbye. 'Please, Uncle Donald,' they begged. 'Let us come with you.'

But Donald shook his head. 'Sorry boys,' he said. 'This mountain climbing is only for experts like me. You stay here.' Then he waved goodbye to his three, very sad nephews.

Guide Goofy walked briskly up the track. Poor Donald followed, huffing and puffing under his heavy load. 'Somebody must have slipped a tonne of lead into this pack,' he grumbled.

Up, up, up they climbed. Goofy went so fast that he pulled Donald along behind him. Finally Goofy came to a steep cliff. He hammered steel spikes into the rock for footholds, making rock chips fall on Donald.

'Hey watch what you're doing!' shouted Donald. He lost his hold on the rock and went spinning out into space on the rope that tied them together. Sharp rocks spattered all around him. He shook his hammer at Goofy. 'Call yourself a guide?' he shouted.

Suddenly the rope carried Donald under a rocky ledge. He quickly hammered a steel spike into the rock to get a foothold, then he began to climb up. But just as he pulled himself up over the rocky ledge, snow began to fall.

'What do you know,' said Goofy. 'It's snowing.'

'Yes I know,' snapped Donald. 'I can see it.'

Donald strapped on his skis and started up the slope behind Goofy.

They had not gone far when Goofy's climbing stick hit a huge ball of snow. Down rolled the snowball, knocking Donald flat on his back and covering him with snow.

Back at the inn, Huey, Dewey and Louie went ice-skating. Then they had fun sledging, but after a while they became restless and decided to look round the village. In the square, they saw a big sign that said: CABLE CAR TO THE MOUNTAIN TOP. Digging down into their pockets they found just enough money to buy tickets for the cable car, and soon they were sailing high above the village.

As they waved to the people below, Huey said, 'This is the life.'

'It certainly beats climbing,' Dewey agreed.

Swaying back and forth, the little car climbed steadily toward the faraway mountain peak. The boys felt as if they were flying. Far below they could see two tiny figures struggling up the mountain but they did not realize that they were their Uncle Donald and his guide, Goofy.

'Look at those silly people,' said Huey. 'They must have started a long time ago. I bet we'll beat them to the top.'

When the cable car slid into the station at the mountain peak, the nephews raced out of the car and up the stairs to the lookout tower. Huey grabbed the long, black telescope and pointed it at the two tiny figures on the slope down below. One of the tiny figures was Uncle Donald, covered with a snowball and a very surprised mountain goat! The other figure was Guide Goofy stuck in a snowbank up to his waist.

The three boys rushed off to the supply hut as fast as they could go. Back they came with a long, stout rope. Huey tied one end of the rope round the railing on the lookout tower, and threw the rest over the edge. Down, down it fell, coil after coil, until it reached the climbers far below.

Tugging with all their might, Huey, Dewey and Louie managed to pull the two frozen mountain climbers up to the top of the lookout tower. Goofy looked round in amazement. 'Gosh!' he said. This is really a great view. I've never climbed to the top of a mountain before.'

When Uncle Donald heard Goofy say that, he was too angry to speak. Squawking with rage, he threw his climbing equipment in all directions. Then, with a great shove, he pushed Goofy off the peak into the snow far below. 'Now that you've seen the peak,' he shouted, 'take a good look at the bottom.' And he marched off with his nephews to get the cable car down.

'This is really fun,' Donald's nephews shouted as the cable car swung back and forth. 'Look at that view, Uncle Donald. Doesn't this feel just like a flying ship?'

Poor Uncle Donald was feeling too sick to answer.

'We love the mountains,' said Huey. 'Can we come up this one again tomorrow?'

Uncle Donald shook his fists with rage. The great mountain climber never wanted to see another mountain as long as he lived!

Huey, Dewey and Louie Beat the Drum

Daisy Duck had given Donald's three nephews a drum each for their birthday.

'Wow! What a wonderful present!' cried Huey, shrieking with delight.

'Terrific!' roared Dewey.

'Smashing!' whooped Louie.

The next morning, they woke up really early and began to play their drums. BOOM! BOOM! BOOM!

'Oh no,' groaned Donald, and he burrowed deep into his bed and pulled the pillows over his head. He twisted and turned but he couldn't sleep. 'Be quiet,' he shouted at his nephews. But they didn't hear him as they were making so much noise!

The boys played the drums all morning, and all afternoon, and all evening, until poor Donald's head echoed – BOOM! BOOM! BOOM!

The next morning, when Huey, Dewey and Louie woke, the first thing they thought of was their drums.

'Hey! My drumsticks have gone!' cried Huey.

'So have mine!' wailed Dewey.

'Mine too!' bellowed Louie. 'We can't possibly play our drums without any drumsticks!'

The boys searched and searched but it was no good. The drums were there but no drumsticks.

Just then, Donald put his head round their bedroom door and smiled smugly. 'I know you can't play your drums without drumsticks. That's why I took them away! I wanted some peace and quiet!' And he went back to bed, feeling very pleased with himself. 'They will never find their drumsticks,' he thought. 'They are safely hidden – in the dustbin.' Then out loud he shouted, 'Remember! No more drumsticks!'

Huey and Dewey looked miserable, but Louie smiled at them. He had an idea. 'Cheer up!' he said. 'Let's go out to Grandma Duck's farm for the day.'

So Huey, Dewey and Louie went over to the farm.

'Hmmm!' sniffed Louie at the farmhouse door. 'It smells as if Grandma has been making toffee apples. I hope we can have some.'

'Not for me,' said Dewey. 'Her toffee is always so hard you can't bite into it!'

'Don't worry about the hardness.' whispered Louie. 'If Grandma says you can have one, take one.' He looked as if he had a big secret.

Just then, Grandma Duck came out. 'Hello my dears,' she beamed. 'Come in. You are just in time to try one of my fresh toffee apples.'

The boys took a toffee apple each. Then, much to Huey and Dewey's surprise, Louie said, 'If we weed your garden, Grandma, can we each have another toffee apple?'

'Of course you can,' smiled Grandma. 'That's a very good idea.'

Grandma Duck thought she had got

a very good bargain. But Huey and Dewey didn't think they had. Now they had to eat two awful toffee apples *and* work.

At last the garden was free of weeds. The three boys went back to the house and Grandma gave them each another apple. 'But you haven't eaten the other apples yet,' she said.

'We're going to take them home,' explained Louie.

'Well, thank you all very much for doing my weeding,' said Grandma.

'I still don't understand why you wanted these toffee apples,' grumbled Dewey to Louie.

Louie then whispered something to his brothers and they all collapsed in a fit of giggles.

Meanwhile, Donald was enjoying a quiet time at home. With no drums banging he could relax quietly, and he settled back in his chair to have a nap.

BOOM! BOOM! BOOM!

Donald leapt out of his chair with a yell. He couldn't believe it and couldn't understand how his nephews had managed to find their drumsticks. He rushed upstairs to their bedroom and flung open the door. There were Huey, Dewey and Louie beating their drums – with toffee apples!

'You said no drumsticks, Uncle Donald,' giggled Huey.

'You didn't say anything about toffee apples, though,' laughed Dewey.

'They sound great don't they?' said Louie.

Poor Donald groaned. Then he had an idea. 'Well, two can play at that game,' he muttered. He threw on his clothes and rushed off to town.

Early the next morning, the triplets were woken by a fearful noise. TWANG! TWANG! TWANG! They stumbled into Donald's room to see what was going on. Donald was playing an electric guitar – very badly.

'What a din!' cried Louie.

'Oh please stop,' begged Huey.

'You're hurting my ears!' said Dewey.

'I'll tell you what,' said Donald at last. 'I won't play my guitar again if you promise not to play your drums.'

Huey, Dewey and Louie had no choice but to agree to the deal. And every morning after that there was peace and quiet in Donald's house.